Contents

NATURE CONSERVANCY COUNCIL

Nature conservation in Great Britain

Preface

It is as a challenge that we introduce 'Nature conservation in Great Britain', the Nature Conservancy Council's contribution to the United Kingdom's response to the World Conservation Strategy. **Nature Conservation in Great Britain** is produced in two parts. One is a summary statement for action. The main publication analyses today's problems and thus provides the rationale for dealing with them against the background of a full review of the progress of conservation over the last few decades so that our experience will help us to plan for the future. Our work is the result of consultation and co-operation between the voluntary bodies and the Nature Conservancy Council as well as with the organisations whose activities affect the practice of nature conservation in this country and overseas.

The first discussion draft was widely distributed for comment in the autumn of 1983 to all bodies concerned with land use and nature conservation and to a number of academic establishments. We were greatly heartened by the evidence of wide commitment to nature conservation shown in the responses we received. A list of those who have commented is given in Annex 2. We thank them for their views, even when there are instances where we have not been able to incorporate them or where we disagree with them.

Because of the very breadth of what concerns nature conservation today, it would be unreasonable to expect full agreement from all parties on all points. It is our hope nonetheless that the document will provide the framework within which action can be taken by all who may be concerned. By doing so they will know that their own particular efforts will be contributing significantly to a determined and co-ordinated programme for nature conservation in this country.

We particularly welcome the endorsement of this strategy which has been received from the voluntary bodies listed on page 6 engaged in nature conservation since they are key partners with the NCC in translating the strategy into action in their various fields.

We are delighted that the Countryside Commission and the Countryside Commission for Scotland welcome the strategy as a clear statement of priorities for nature conservation and that where objectives and interests coincide, the Commissions look forward to co-operating closely with NCC. Additionally we are particularly pleased that the Royal Botanic Gardens (Kew) welcome the general thrust of this document especially concerning those themes related to its functions.

I must also pay tribute to the work of Derek Ratcliffe who has borne the greater part of the burden in producing what I believe to be a classic work that should be instrumental in determining the future of our countryside for which he has striven so hard throughout his working life.

The importance of this document will be decided by the amount of constructive discussion and the actions that follow from it. We, at the NCC, intend to play our full part both directly and wherever appropriate by working through and stimulating other bodies and individuals — whether to extend their good work or to take new initiatives to conserve our wildlife heritage. Yet it is people everywhere who will determine our success or failure. We therefore address this strategy to government, which sets the social and economic stage upon which nature conservation has to play its part, and to local government and community councils. We direct our suggestions to farmers and landowners whose role as the custodians of so much of our national heritage, is vital. We seek the support of the scientific world whose researches are so important in determining the measures appropriate and necessary for the future. We wish to enlist the help of all caring people who show their love of our wildlife and wild places in steadily increasing numbers. Finally we invite our fellows in the conservation movement to join with us in putting our recommendations into effect. It is a challenge which none of us must shirk.

William Wilkinson
Chairman NCC
26 April 1984

Non-governmental organisations endorsing the
strategy
*Animal Welfare Institute
*Biology Curators Group
*British Association of Nature Conservationists
 British Ecological Society
*British Herpetological Society
*British Naturalists' Association
*Botanical Society of the British Isles
 Council for Environmental Education
*Conservation Society
 Council for the Preservation of Rural England
 Farming and Wildlife Advisory Group
*Flora and Fauna Preservation Society
*Field Studies Council
*Friends of the Earth
*Green Alliance
*International Council for Bird Preservation
*International Fund for Animal Welfare
*International League for the Protection
     of Cetaceans
*Joint Committee for the Conservation of
     British Insects
 National Trust
 National Trust for Scotland
*People's Trust for Endangered Species
*Ramblers Association
*Royal Society for Protection of Birds
*Royal Society for Nature Conservation
 Scottish Wildlife Trust
*Underwater Conservation Society
*Vincent Wildlife Trust
*Wildfowl Trust
*World Wildlife Fund — UK
*Woodland Trust
*Youth Hostels Association
*Zoological Society of London

*Member or observer organisations of
Wildlife Link

Introduction

Man is a part of nature, but the conservation of nature has come to be understood as the regulation of human use of the global ecosystem to sustain its diversity of content indefinitely. Mankind has come to dominate nature through a ruthless exploitation of its resources, to the point where permanent damage and depletion are all too obvious. Some physical components, notably fossil fuels, are not renewable and when exhausted can only be replaced by substitutes. Others, especially the organisms that provide all our food, are infinitely renewable if managed appropriately and in harmony with the soils and waters on which they depend. If human populations grow too large or occupy harsh and unproductive environments, they all too easily outstrip the capacity of the land to support them, with results so tragically familiar in some countries. Conservation seeks to relieve and avoid such problems, and to instil good housekeeping principles into resource management for the material benefit of everyone.

But man does not live by bread alone. Civilisation has brought leisure and the need for people to find fulfilment of the spirit as well as the body. Increasingly, they turn to the out-of-doors to nourish their minds, finding interest, inspiration and enjoyment in a wide variety of ways. And that pursuit of knowledge we call science finds boundless scope in the natural world. Whether this perception of nature is profound or simple, it belongs to the range of concern which is within the developing culture of human society. Nature is thus a resource of another kind, with a non-material quality which supports the spiritual advancement of mankind. The conservation of nature to maintain its bounty for this purpose has to be set alongside concern to sustain its value as a material asset, though these two strands become interwoven.

The World Conservation Strategy (WCS) spelt out these issues and the need to address them on the global scale. Britain's land-use has been of a generally conserving kind in supplying the material needs of its people, though this has been helped by the fortunate circumstances of a benign climate. This is, however, a heavily or even an over-populated country, and sustaining a population of fifty-four million people on 230,000 sq km of land at a high standard of living can hardly be achieved without considerable pressure on natural assets. Conservation problems here are becoming more acute, and the recently published **Conservation and Development Programme for the UK** (1983) proposes a wide approach to them. **Nature Conservation in Great Britain** is a statement of the way in which organisations, official and non-official, and individuals concerned with the conservation of wildlife and physical features can

contribute to this Programme for natural resource management and use. By linking our more specialised programme to the Conservation and Development Programme with its wider scope, we seek to ensure that the conservation of nature is carried forward within the broader context of the wise use of natural resources, as the founders of post-war nature conservation intended.

The nature conservation movement in Britain has made great strides during the second half of this century and has substantial achievements to its credit. Enthusiasm for nature is now a major concern of our society, and there is a wide appreciation of conservation principles and needs. Nevertheless, although nature has become a major public interest, many feel that its conservation has reached a critical time. Other uses of the natural environment create an adverse impact on its wild flora, fauna and physical features, and the continuing depletion of this national heritage is causing growing anxiety. The richness of this heritage owes much to those who occupied and managed the land in the past, and nature conservation will continue to be greatly dependent on sympathetic attitudes on the part of all land-users. There is, however, justifiable alarm that economic forces and policies are increasingly pressing the managers of land and other natural resources into practices inimical to the conservation of nature. This country has hitherto been regarded as one of the world's leaders in providing for the care of wild nature, but, as these irreplaceable assets suffer continuing erosion, there is some danger of this reputation becoming tarnished if not lost.

Nature Conservation in Great Britain examines such problems and sets out a strategy for dealing with them. Its audience is wide. It speaks to and for those whose primary concern is with nature conservation, by providing a statement of intent on their behalf; it addresses all those whose interests and activities particularly impinge upon nature, showing them what is proposed and how they can contribute to the programme; and lastly it appeals to the nation at large, notably through its elected representatives in parliament and government, to acknowledge its responsibility to the conservation of nature and to provide for this accordingly.

Strategy is understood to be a definition of the main framework of approaches to meet basic objectives. A formulation of a nature conservation strategy for Great Britain has to be set in the context of both past and present, especially in relation to objectives and desired results. Aims have evolved over several decades and need to be redefined for the future. A brief historical background and a discussion of achievements thus preface the proposals for a joint governmental and non-government strategy to carry nature conservation forward into the twenty-first century. The strategy is built around existing legislation, but if further experience shows present measures to be inadequate in meeting objectives, then further strengthening of the law will become necessary.

Finally, it must be recognised that government has a crucial role in setting the social, environmental, agricultural, industrial and economic policy framework within which all those concerned with nature conservation have to operate in order to achieve their objectives. Government holds the scales, and ultimately it will have to decide where it wishes the balance between nature conservation and other sectional interests to lie. And the view taken by government, in representing the people, will depend on its perception of public concern.

Part I Aims, methods and achievements of nature conservation in Great Britain

1 The origins of conservation in Britain

1.1 The story of human occupation of the land has been one of increasing transformation of the original state of nature. During the last 2,000 years, enormous ecological change has been wrought on the face of Britain; the great spreads of primeval forest and the swamps of the wetter lowlands have largely been removed. In their place is the twentieth century landscape, in the lowlands divided largely between farmland and the built environment and in the uplands composed mainly of treeless rough grazings. The remaining scatter of ancient woodlands is at best only semi-natural, and most of that re-created during the present century is largely artificial.

1.2 Yet the sense of need to protect some of the ancient habitat also has a long history. Hunting sanctuaries established by the Anglo-Saxon and Norman kings remain as some of the most important wildlife areas today, and the numerous game preserves and fox coverts of a later age have helped to maintain scattered woodlands in the agricultural lowlands. The owners of large estates developed and set standards of scenic appreciation in their parklands and also replanted woodland extensively for economic reasons. The management of many northern moorlands principally for game slowed the relentless onslaught of the sheep and maintained large areas of dwarf shrub heath instead of grassland. And the large number and extent of commons in England and Wales kept at bay some of the reclamation and development which have been so damaging to wild nature.

1.3 During this long period there developed concern to manage the land so as to maintain its productivity, both for the immediate future and for generations to come. There evolved down the centuries the tradition of care and stewardship for the land by those who lived upon it. Land, with its crops, livestock and timber, came to be understood as a vital resource, whose bounty was sustained by knowledge of management handed down as a living inheritance. Thus it was that conservation became a fundamental principal of land-use long before the word itself came to be understood in its present sense. In so far as the wild mammals, birds and fish represented a valued resource of food, game and sport, they also were included within the concept.

1.4 Concern for scenic and landscape values began to influence human modifications of the land from the eighteenth century onwards, but concern for the conservation of nature in the presently understood sense is barely one hundred years old. Indeed, until land began to be managed with conscious intent to protect its wildlife, from around 1900 onwards, it could fairly be said that our heritage of nature had survived by accident rather than design. While it is true that the transformation of scene over two millennia left — or even created — a still rich and valued range of habitats, wild flora and fauna and physical features, their occurrence was largely incidental to the other purposes for which the land was managed. The wish to protect and sustain populations of wild plants and animals because of a wider concern for nature as a scientific and aesthetic resource is the most modern facet of this evolving view of conservation, and it is with this aspect that the present report deals in particular.

2 Development of the nature conservation movement

2.1 The nature conservation movement in this stricter sense began in this country with the early attempts at bird protection in the mid nineteenth century by the Royal Society for the Prevention of Cruelty to Animals (RSPCA) and the passing of the first Bird Protection Act in 1869. A local society established a bird reserve at Breydon Water in 1888, and a year later the Society for the Protection of Birds (later the Royal Society for Protection of Birds — RSPB) was created. The National Trust was set up in 1895 and by 1910 owned 13 sites with wildlife importance. The Society for the Preservation of the Wild Fauna of the Empire was founded in 1903: now renamed the Fauna and Flora Preservation Society, it has throughout its existence been concerned mainly with the conservation of terrestrial vertebrates. In 1910 Charles Rothschild established the nature reserve at Woodwalton Fen, and then with three other enthusiasts he founded the Society for the Promotion of Nature Reserves (SPNR) in 1912. By 1915, the Society had compiled a countrywide list of 251 areas of national importance for wildlife, of which 52 were recommended as nature reserves. The Society's emphasis was on promotion of action by others, but, following Rothschild's untimely death in 1923, little progress was made with further acquisitions. Certain private landowners also began in these early years to try to reverse the effects of the excesses of game preserving, and then of egg collecting, on some of the rarest birds, notable examples being the work on protection of the red kite in Wales and of Broadland predators and tern colonies in Norfolk.

2.2 Beyond the concern for wildlife protection, there was still longer-standing curiosity about natural history, which grew during the nineteenth century and was expressed especially in the collecting of specimens. Numerous societies dealing with botany, zoology, geology or general natural history were formed, and attracted both professional and amateur membership. The Royal Society, as the premier scientific organisation, supported the advancement of knowledge in these fields, notably through the universities and other learned institutions. The British Ecological Society, founded in 1911, was composed mainly of professional scientists. Many of the leading thinkers in the developing conservation movement were university scientists, but some of the prime movers were exceptional individuals in a variety of other spheres. Through the energies of one such group, the British Trust for Ornithology (BTO) was formed in 1933 with a staff to promote scientific bird studies, guiding and co-ordinating the efforts of the growing number of amateur ornithologists.

2.3 In 1941 the SPNR again took the initiative in calling a conference to consider Nature Preservation in Post-War Reconstruction, and this recommended setting up the Nature Reserves Investigation Committee. Leading amateurs and professionals in the field of natural history came together to launch the movement which government subsequently embraced. There followed the Wild Life Conservation Special Committee (England and Wales), composed of leading ecologists, biologists and earth scientists under the chairmanship first of Sir Julian Huxley and later of Sir Arthur Tansley. This distinguished company represented a much larger body of relevant scientific opinion, located especially in the Royal Society and the British Ecological Society and other learned bodies. Their report, **Conservation of Nature in England and Wales** (Cmd 7122, 1947), contains a remarkable distillation of constructive thinking, in which a clear exposition of rationale is linked to specific recommendations for a practical development programme.

2.4 This rationale elegantly presents an integrated concept of nature conservation, which envisages that the natural renewable resources of the country should be developed yet sustained for the manifold benefit of society, through the application of scientific insight to management and control. Research would expand knowledge about the attributes and processes of nature, thereby contributing to the advancement of science, as well as informing practical conservation action. Natural phenomena were valued for a variety of purposes — scientific, educational, aesthetic and economic. The concept embraced biological subjects and the physical environment, with geological and physiographic features accorded intrinsic importance. Nature reserves were to be a key part of the action programme, with their purposes enlarged beyond the earlier idea of wildlife sanctuaries, to include use as research and experimental areas but also for education and enjoyment.

2.5 This concept of nature conservation as primarily a scientific activity in both methods and objectives developed in parallel with that of use of the countryside as an aesthetic and recreational resource. The two concerns were seen to be interwoven and mutually supportive. The setting-up of National Parks, as the cornerstone to the aesthetic approach, would require management advice based on the fruits of survey and ecological research, and the Parks would themselves contain areas and features of especial value and relevance to the conduct of such studies. The proposal to establish a Biological Service as the agency for nature conservation was firmly linked to the research, management advice and nature reserve functions, but was intended to contribute also to the countryside recreation programme. Moreover, the Wild Life Conservation Special Committee was actually set up, with overlapping membership, by the National Parks Committee (England and Wales), and the reports of both committees were published simultaneously in July 1947. That year also saw the publication of Cmd 7235, **National Parks and the Conservation of Nature in Scotland,** to be followed in 1949 by **Final Report on Nature Reserves in Scotland** (Cmd 7814).

2.6 It was thus as a result of the initiative and drive within the voluntary sector that nature conservation gained governmental acceptance and support, and so become part of parliamentary concern for the affairs of the nation. Official recognition of nature conservation through the establishment of the Nature Conservancy and the passing of the National Parks and Access to the Countryside Act in 1949 in turn gave new impetus and leadership to the voluntary bodies. For the sake of clarity, the history of development of the official and the voluntary bodies for nature conservation is treated separately, since a strictly chronological account would be less easy to follow.

3.1 The proposal for a Biological Service was given effect by the creation of the Nature Conservancy (NC) in 1949. The new body was established by Royal Charter, under the aegis of a Committee of the Privy Council, and given statutory powers and duties by the National Parks and Access to the Countryside Act 1949. Its functions as summarised in the Charter were:
"To provide scientific advice on the conservation and control of the natural flora and fauna of Great Britain; to establish, maintain and manage nature reserves in Great Britain, including maintenance of physical features of scientific interest; and to organise and develop the research and scientific services related thereto."
Responsibility for Northern Ireland was specifically omitted.

3.2 The Nature Conservancy, as a governing committee, was composed mainly of distinguished scientists, and during the formative years 1952-1965 it had the inspired leadership of Max Nicholson as Director General. There were supporting committees, of which those for Scotland, England, Wales, Scientific Policy and Grants were the most important. Headquarters for Scotland and Wales were established in Edinburgh and Bangor, the Great Britain Headquarters being in London. Scientifically qualified staff were recruited into two groups, one concerned with research and the other with the executive work of nature conservation. Geographically dispersed research stations were developed around the first group, while the second group was organised according to a countrywide geographical subdivision into regions under the appropriate headquarters.

3.3 The Charter functions and the duty laid upon the NC to notify Sites of Special Scientific Interest (SSSIs) to planning authorities amounted to a three-pronged strategy for nature conservation. The most directly executive part was to safeguard important areas, notably by establishing and managing a national series of nature reserves. The advisory role was partly promotional and partly responsive. The third function, of developing research and scientific services, was similar to that of a Research Council. Administrative arrangements were, in fact, changed in

1965 by transferring the NC from the aegis of the Privy Council Committee to the newly constituted Natural Environment Research Council (NERC) funded through the Department of Education and Science.

3.4 National Nature Reserves

3.4.1 Policy in establishing a national series of nature reserves followed closely the concepts and proposals in Cmd 7122. Such reserves were to be the means of protecting, in perpetuity and through appropriate control and management, the most important areas of natural or semi-natural vegetation, with their characteristic flora, fauna and controlling environmental conditions, and notable geological and physiographic features. These areas were chosen as examples giving an adequate representation of the countrywide range of variation in such natural phenomena — the biological reserves partly for their representation of habitats and communities and partly for their species complements. The 73 proposed National Nature Reserves (NNRs), together with a further 24 for Scotland, became the list for acquisition.

3.4.2 The NNR acquisition programme grew rapidly by purchase of freehold of the land through the NC's Grant-in-Aid, negotiation of leases with owners, or formal agreement with owners and occupiers on mutually acceptable management. When a reserve was established, it was customary to appoint a warden as custodian, guide, manager and recorder. Management plans were prepared for reserves, and recording of environmental and biological data was instituted, with later addition of records of events relevant to management.

3.4.3 The NNRs were variably utilised as study areas for research. Some, such as Moor House and Rhum, became the focus for extensive research programmes by both Conservancy and university scientists, but others received little attention. Much of the reserve management work was concerned with the restoration of woodland and with the tenance of chalk and limesto grasslands and of fens by grazing or cut water regim were controlled and apparatus set up with less risk of damage than elsewhere.

3.4.4 By 1973, 135 NNRs totalling 112,723 hectares (278,537 acres) had been established. Many of the original 97 proposals were included, but some of these proved intractable or were not pursued for other reasons such as adequacy of existing safeguard. The acquisitions also added many other important areas which were either overlooked in Cmd 7122 and Cmd 7814 or placed there in a category which did not receive statutory recognition in the 1949 legislation. A few of the reserves were large, with areas over 3,000 ha, but most were less than 500 ha in extent.

3.5 Sites of Special Scientific Interest

3.5.1 The SSSI series formed a national network complementing and extending the NNR series by adding a larger number of areas judged worthy of protection for their nature conservation importance. Planning applications affecting SSSIs were referred to the NC, and handling these became a significant part of the regional tasks. Increasingly, conflict between development and nature conservation interests on SSSIs was resolved through public inquiries, with NC regional staff acting as expert witnesses or objectors. From 1968 onwards, the NC was able to make Management Agreements with owners of SSSIs, which rested mainly on goodwill shown by farmers and other land-users towards nature conservation needs, but could provide payments for actual work involved. Few such agreements were concluded because of shortage of funds.

3.5.2 The SSSI device gradually proved to be a more effective means of safeguarding important areas than had originally seemed likely. It nevertheless had basic weaknesses, notably owing to the exclusion of agricultural and forestry developments from planning law, and many SSSIs were damaged or completely destroyed through such activities. By 1973, some 3,500 SSSIs had been notified, the majority for biological interest, but several hundred for their geological or physiographic features.

3.6 A Nature Conservation Review

3.6.1 The identification of further areas as either potential reserves or SSSIs depended on extensive new fieldwork. The enthusiasm of Cmd 7122 for survey of the biological and physical resources of Britain did not, however, carry over into the established science policy of the NC. Recognition of the need for such survey revived when the NNR programme was appraised and seen to be based on only a partial knowledge of important wildlife areas and physical features. Concern to ensure a more adequate NNR series and to forecast the probable resource and other practical implications led in 1966 to the launching of **A Nature Conservation Review** (NCR) to identify the areas of national biological importance to nature conservation in Britain. Although the results were not published until 1977, the NCR had by 1970 listed 735 such areas, including nearly all the existing NNRs. These 'key sites' were described in some detail, and their selection was set against a background account of the total range of variation in wildlife and its habitats in Britain, together with a rationale for evaluating nature conservation interest in this whole field. The methods of safeguard were not prescribed, but it was made clear that each key site deserved protection equivalent to that afforded by NNR designation. NCC decided as policy to notify them all as SSSIs, though the process is not yet quite complete.

3.7 The advisory role

3.7.1 The SSSI mechanism spanned two main prongs of conservation strategy, namely a site safeguard process achieved through an advisory approach, since protection of these sites depended largely on representations to planners and owners and occupiers over proposed developments. The rest of the conservation programme, dealing with the larger part of Britain outside the NNRs and SSSIs, had to rely mainly on development of the advisory and persuasion role. This involved making contacts with central and local government, public utilities and other bodies, non-government organisations, learned institutions, groups and individuals whose responsibilities and activities particularly impinged on the land and nature, so as to achieve understanding and gain sympathy when interests were in competition or conflict.

3.7.2 A main objective was to infuse ecological and conservation thinking into the attitudes and actions of all those concerned with the use of land and other natural resources. Advice was also available in response to requests for help over conservation and management problems relating to renewable resources and over any other issues in which an ecological viewpoint was desirable. There was particularly close liaison with planning authorities, as their strategic role became increasingly important in determining patterns of development. A countrywide network of connections, both formal and informal and at all levels, was gradually built up. An advisory role also developed with regard to operation of the laws concerning or affecting nature conservation and to any revision of such legislation.

3.7.3 To support this role, an information, publicity and educational service was developed with the NC. Suitable opportunities for promoting the conservation message were sought within the educational system and the media, and inputs made to museums, exhibitions, shows and information centres. Talks and lectures became an important staff activity, and these ranged from technical papers read to learned institutions to more popular expositions to natural history societies and non-scientific groups. Wardens helped to inform the public on NNRs, and on some of them guided walks and nature trails were established. The growing public interest in nature was fostered in various ways, and the development of the voluntary sector encouraged.

3.8 Research

3.8.1 The Conservancy was set up with some of the functions of a Research Council in ecology. By 1973, it had established eight research stations, staffed by nearly 200 scientists. Research activity ranged from basic studies, aimed largely at the advancement of science, to applied work planned to provide direct support over pressing conservation issues in reserve management and wildlife problems in the wider countryside. One major theme was production ecology and nutrient cycling, which gave the Conservancy a major role in the International Biological Programme. Another was the work of the Toxic Chemicals and Wildlife Research Section aimed at providing data and advice on wildlife-pesticide problems through the Government's Advisory Committee on Pesticides and other Toxic Chemicals. The work of the Red Grouse Unit illustrated the attention given to a single wild species with considerable economic importance. Most themes which began as applied research also made substantial contributions to science.

3.8.2 The bulk of the research was biological, and fairly evenly divided between botanical and zoological studies. Need for analysis of soils, waters, plants and animals for mineral nutrient and organic content, and later for measurement of toxic chemical residues, led to development of chemical laboratory services. The relevance of coastal physiographic processes, soil conditions and climatology to the NC's interests resulted in the development of small research units with relevant expertise. A team of statisticians handled the growing demand for help over experimental design and data analysis, and computer technology was increasingly used to facilitate information handling and storage. A Biological Records Centre was established to collect data on species

distribution. The main lines of research were guided by the Scientific Policy Committee.

3.8.3 The research activities eventually covered much of the field of nature conservation which needed the support of scientific and technical information and advice. There was a tendency for conservation on reserves and SSSIs to focus on habitat and community management, while the approach in the wider environment was often orientated towards species. This was reflected in research developments. While the research arm developed into a wide-ranging ecological studies institute, a freshwater group was not formed until 1966; and there was no remit for dealing with marine conservation below low tide level. One later development was the organisation of survey and management expertise into Habitat Teams which contained 'user' interest in the form of regional staff.

3.8.4 Support was given to university and other outside research, mainly through grants to meritorious applicants for postgraduate research degrees and assistantships to more senior workers. Projects were judged on scientific merit and/or on relevance to nature conservation, so that support was again for a wide spectrum from basic to applied research. Awards were usually of two to four years' duration, but some longer-term grants were given to teams of scientists developing particular fields of study, such as the research arms of the Wildfowl Trust and British Trust for Ornithology, the Unit of Animal Behaviour at Oxford University and the Botanical Society of the British Isles for its plant distribution mapping scheme. The development of university MSc courses in conservation and ecology was supported by studentship awards at University College London, Bangor, Durham and Aberdeen. From 1965 this function was incorporated within the wider university support role of NERC, though the NC retained responsibility for funding of terrestrial life sciences.

3.9 Geology and physiography

A small team of earth scientists was recruited to deal with the conservation of physical features. Their work focussed on the more fragile features important to earth science education and research, such as type localities for series of rock strata with classic sections (often manmade, in quarries and cuttings), major fossil-bearing beds, geological discontinuities showing earth movements, erosional features such as karst systems and caves, rare rock types and minerals, glacial and periglacial features such as morainic and solifluction forms, and landforms created by inland water action and by the sea. Much of the work consisted of ensuring that the most important features were identified, described and notified as SSSIs and then monitored for threat of development and damage. This involved building up a liaison network within the community of earth scientists outside the NC and obtaining their help. The NC staff then had to handle the many cases of conflicting interest which arose through planning applications, and they gave frequent assistance to their regional colleagues in resulting public inquiries. Although Figure 1 and Annex 1:1 distinguish between physical feature and biological SSSIs, many sites have overlapping interest and are important for both. More recently, NCC has embarked on the restoration of geological sites and the digging of new sections by use of mechanical excavators.

ments, notably through the promotion of international conventions. The Conservancy developed connections with the conservation work of the Council of Europe and supported bodies such as the International Waterfowl Research Bureau (IWRB), International Council for Bird Preservation (ICBP) and International Union of Game Biologists (IUGB), as well as international congresses in relevant subjects. It encouraged exchange visits with other countries and now and then seconded officers to work on Commonwealth conservation projects.

Figure 1: Categories of protected area for nature conservation

Category	Number	Area in hectares
National Nature Reserve	195	150,003
RSPB Reserve	93	43,728
Nature Conservation Trust Reserve	c.1,400	44,090
Woodland Trust Reserve	102	1,214
Forest Nature Reserve	11	2,448
Local Nature Reserve	105	14,371
Wildfowl Refuges additional to those covered by other categories	44	11,180
		266,034
Bird sanctuaries	16	—
Biological SSSI	3,166 ⎱ 4,150*	1,470,900
Geological SSSI	984 ⎰	

*including those covered by other listed categories

3.10   **International work**
3.10.1 The last main area of activity was in international conservation, notably in supporting the International Union for Conservation of Nature and Natural Resources (IUCN), of which NCC is a UK member. Conservation problems are much the same across the world, and they differ mainly in degree, scale and rate. Experience and expertise are thus valuably shared, and IUCN became an important forum for discussion and exchange of information, as well as a means of influencing national govern-

4 The Nature Conservancy Council, 1973-1984

4.1 In 1973, growing stresses from the NC's uneasy relocation as a promotional agency within a Research Council coincided with government acceptance of 'customer-contractor' arrangements for applied research and development. The NC was accordingly split by the Nature Conservancy Council Act, the executive part being reconstituted as an independent Council (NCC) funded through the Department of the Environment, while the research arm remained in NERC as the Institute of Terrestrial Ecology (ITE). Government Ministers stressed the significance of the decision to give the new NCC this degree of autonomy, so that it could take a strong and independent line on major issues when necessary.

4.2 NCC was given reduced funds with which to commission research, though the Act also conferred the power to conduct its own research as appropriate. The research programme necessarily contracted considerably and became limited to work of practical application to urgent conservation problems, with emphasis on survey. Although ITE continued to conduct a great deal of strategic research in nature conservation, the ready availability of its scientific advice steadily declined. NCC appointed a Chief Scientist and supporting team to manage the commissioned research programme, but the internal demand for advice became so great that this group became primarily a scientific advisory service to the whole organisation.

4.3 NCC retained much of its previous structure otherwise, but it added an England Headquarters in Banbury. Regional commands were strengthened to cope with the increasing demands of site conservation and the advisory workload. NCC's **Statement of Policies** published in November 1974 set out the areas of conservation activity and their objectives. New responsibilities appeared in connection with flora and fauna legislation and new problems from national development of energy sources. A new power to give grants became an important instrument of NCC policy particularly in supporting the development of the NGOs by funds for purchase and management of land as nature reserves, recruitment of professional staff, promotional work and support for a variety of practical activities. The NNR acquisition programme was maintained, and a Geological Conservation Review launched to identify sites with physical features of national importance. Biological survey was so continuous and integral a need for NCC that funds from the research programme were translated into permanent internal surveyor posts grouped into three Country Field Units.

4.4 The need to amend UK legislation to conform to obligations on government stemming from the EEC and other international sources led to the Wildlife and Countryside Act 1981. This had four main elements of great importance to NCC. The first was a strengthening of the law protecting wild birds and other animals and wild plants, with the addition of further endangered species to the special schedules, including all British species of bat. The second was the creation of powers to establish Marine Nature Reserves (MNRs). The third and most controversial element was a revision of the measures for site safeguard to give powers to protect any SSSI coming under threat, subject to compensation for profit forgone in withdrawing proposed agricultural or forestry development. The fourth provided for protection of limestone pavements.

4.5 The 1981 Act imposed extra duties on NCC. The new wildlife protection provisions led to the transfer of the functions of the government's Advisory Committees on the Protection of Birds to NCC and extended the provisions for licensing the taking of birds and other animals. At the same time NCC was appointed the Scientific Authority for animals endangered in trade, under the terms of the Endangered Species (Import and Export) Act 1976. These are minor burdens compared with the new arrangements for site safeguard, which require renotification of all owners and occupiers of all SSSIs, with a statement of operations likely to be damaging to their nature conservation interest. This has often necessitated resurveying existing sites and their boundaries. There is, moreover, concern to locate all other areas which are of SSSI status, so that these too may be notified under the terms of the 1981 Act. This work has distorted, at least temporarily, the programme of the whole NCC, but especially of regional staff.

4.6 Marine Nature Reserves can now be designated between high water mark and the three-mile territorial limit, by order made by the Secretary of State for the Environment in England (or the appropriate Secretary of State in Scotland and Wales) on the advice of NCC. The intended functions of such reserves are the same as for NNRs but they have been perceived as inimical to other interests and complex consultations and agreement on appropriate byelaws are required before an MNR can be established. NCC is trying to set up, initially, a small number of MNRs over areas of the highest conservation value, whilst monitoring closely just how far in practice effective conservation management can be achieved within the legislation, which tightly circumscribes the controls which NCC can itself place over activities within such reserves.

4.7 NCC presently has a staff of 590 and a Grant-in-Aid of £14·4 million (1984/85). The total number of SSSIs at present stands at 4,150, of which 984 are geological sites, and a further 1,200 sites are being investigated as possible SSSIs. All NCR sites and NNRs will be notified as SSSIs. The total area of SSSIs is about 1·47 million ha, representing 6·5% of the surface of Britain, but with the largest extent in coastal areas and the uplands. The NNR series totals 195, covering an area of 150,000 ha. (Figure 2).

Figure 2: Progress in acquisition of National Nature Reserves

Year	No.	Hectares
1949-1952	9	c.8,903
1953	11	9,105
1954	20	28,795
1955	35	31,985
1956	47	33,453
1957	56	49,303
1958	70	53,858
1959	80	55,765
1960	84	56,250
1961	92	72,413
1962	100	77,172
1963	105	88,276
1964	111	92,414
1965-1966	113	95,277
1067	117	99,749
1968	124	104,105
1969	126	104,781
1970	128	107,286
1971	130	108,719
1972	131	109,837
1973	135	112,724
1973-1975	140	114,514
1976	145	119,585
1977	153	120,465
1978	161	126,246
1979	164	127,312
1980	166	132,555
1981	171	133,640
1982	182	139,078
(March) 1983	189	142,215
(October) 1983	193	146,624

Number of
National Nature Reserves

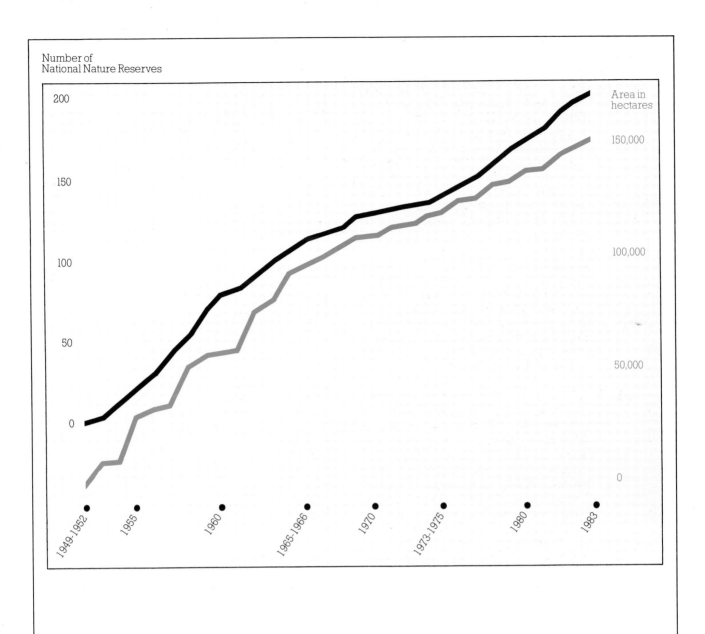

Growth of the NGOs, 1945-1984

5.1   In parallel with the official agency, the non-governmental organisations for nature conservation (NGOs) have developed as the other main arm of the nature conservation movement. Their growth and success have been epitomised by two bodies, the RSPB and the RSNC.

5.2   **Royal Society for the Protection of Birds**
5.2.1 The RSPB took the lead within the voluntary movement and has grown from a small group concerned mainly with legal protection of birds to a large and highly professional organisation with 350 staff and an annual budget of £6·3 million, covering the whole range of bird conservation. The growth of its membership exemplifies the quite dramatic increase in popular enthusiasm for wildlife and its protection. In 1946 there were 6,000 members, and only 8,100 in 1959, but by 1970 there were 65,677 and in 1983 no less than 361,443 with another 96,000 in the Young Ornithologists' Club. The Society led the way in persuading parliament to pass comprehensive legislation in the Protection of Birds Act 1954, and it played a major role in further revisions of this law in 1967 and 1981. Its staff have been the main instrument in the enforcement of this legislation and, through their public relations and educational work, have been especially influential in helping to create a favourable climate of opinion about bird protection within our society. It is particularly through their work that the illegal taking and killing of birds and the collecting of eggs have become regarded as unacceptable activities and the keeping of captive birds and shooting for sport have become strictly controlled.

5.2.2 The RSPB has developed its promotional and public relations role with great success and financial benefit. It has a members' magazine, **Birds,** and a large sales department aimed at raising funds. A film unit produces high quality films on bird life which have an enormous popular appeal. Key problems, such as the illegal international trade in captive birds and the unlawful use of poisons by certain sporting and farming interests to kill predators, have been investigated and reported upon in depth with telling effect. The Society has a research team which studies important conservation problems, and there is a countrywide network of regional officers who maintain an on-the-ground presence and deal with regional or local issues.

5.2.3 One of the most important parts of the RSPB's work, strongly developed in the post-war period, is its nature reserve acquisition programme. There are now 95 bird reserves totalling 47,600 ha, most of SSSI and many of NNR quality, and during the last few years the Society has spent more on the acquisition of reserves than the NCC. These reserves are managed for the wildlife interest in general, as well as for their birds, and normal policy is to arrange public access and viewing facilities, so that they serve a valuable educational and recreational function under the guidance of their wardens. Public relations work is thus closely integrated with active conservation measures. The RSPB has also participated widely in international work and has played a leading role in the support of the International Council for Bird Preservation.

5.3   **Royal Society for Nature Conservation**
5.3.1 The post-war period has seen the parallel growth of the Nature Conservation Trusts. From 1958 the SPNR took over the role of co-ordinating the Trusts' activities and providing common services. Recognition of its importance in this role, and of the Trust movement, came with the granting of a new Royal Charter in 1976 and the change of title to Royal Society for Nature Conservation (RSNC) in 1981. The RSNC now has a headquarters with about 20 full-time staff, runs a sales business and produces a members' magazine, **Natural World,** and a reserves handbook. Its junior arm, WATCH, has more than 14,000 members organised in over 250 area groups centrally serviced by the Society but run by the Trusts.

5.3.2 The RSNC provides the Trusts with a national identity, promotes their common interests, represents their views on national issues, provides a forum for exchange of ideas and experience, and helps in their search for funds. The Society has greatly influenced national conservation policies, most recently through its campaigning for stronger and more comprehensive conservation legislation. It has taken a special interest in the problems of wildlife in relation to agriculture and land drainage, as reflected in its report **Towards 2000 — a Place for Wildlife in a Land-use Strategy.**

5.3.3 The two main NGOs, the RSPB and RSNC, have thus developed a range of functions in some cases similar to and in others complementary to each other's and to the NCC's. All three work closely together, supporting or leading as circumstances indicate.

5.4 The Trusts for Nature Conservation

5.4.1 The Norfolk Naturalists' Trust, founded in 1926, was the first of these bodies which sprang from a realisation of the need to set up new county organisations to carry out and promote nature conservation and attract broad support at the local level. The next Trusts were not founded until 1946 in Yorkshire, and 1948 in Lincolnshire, and for another decade the momentum was slow, so that in 1958 there were still only 1,750 members in ten Trusts. The movement then developed rapidly and 26 years later there were 150,000 members in 46 Trusts covering the whole of the UK.

5.4.2 Under the RSNC's umbrella, the Trusts retain local autonomy and concentration of effort, through both site safeguard and their educational, advisory and information work. Their members have played a large part in the identification of prospective SSSIs and reserves, and in other surveys and recording schemes which link with others such as enquiries by the British Trust for Ornithology and the Biological Records Centre's mapping schemes. The total of Trust reserves now exceeds 1,400 and, though many are small, their total area is around 44,090 ha. More than half of these are SSSIs and 18% are sites equivalent in quality to NNRs. This reserve series covers virtually all habitats, with an extremely wide range of plants and animal communities and species. Management of reserves is an important activity — constrained in many cases by lack of funds, but much assisted lately by Manpower Services Commission help. The educational function of reserves has been developed, with nature trails and interpretative centres an important aspect, and some have been used as research study areas. Trusts have increasingly employed conservation officers and wardens and have become much involved in liaison with local planning authorities and in dealing with public inquiries and the provision of advice to various parties.

5.4.3 The Scottish Wildlife Trust was founded in 1964 to fulfil in Scotland to role of the Naturalists' Trusts in England and Wales. In 1983 the Trust had 8,000 members distributed throughout Scotland.

5.5 Specialist NGOs

5.5.1 The British Trust for Ornithology (BTO) continued to develop essentially as a science-based organisation, undertaking more frequent and ambitious surveys through membership help and developing its research programme and the Bird Ringing Scheme. The NC supported the BTO's research and a full-time Director of Research was appointed. The Trust did not engage in practical field conservation, since the RSPB handled this aspect, but contributed important technical information and advice on conservation issues, notably over the effects of organochlorine pesticides on wild bird populations and on changes in status and distribution. Its journal, **Bird Study,** also became a leading vehicle for scientific papers in ornithology. The BTO had the particular value of creating a bridge between the amateur naturalist and the professional scientist, and its catalytic effect on the energies of its membership was especially fruitful. Appealing especially to the serious ornithologist, it has remained relatively small in numbers (7,000-8,000) but is the envy of many other countries.

5.5.2 In 1946 the Wildfowl Trust was set up to promote the study and conservation of this group of birds around the world. A wildfowl collection for study was built up at Slimbridge, and later captive breeding of internationally endangered species, such as the Hawaiian goose, was undertaken to allow restocking in the wild. The Trust developed a research arm, which engaged in ringing and migration work and species studies, and used amateur help in instituting annual wildfowl counts. Several wildfowl reserves were later acquired and the Trust contributed management and conservation advice on wildfowl generally. The research programme has been funded mainly by grant-aid from the NC, and latterly NCC. The Trust has also played a leading role in the development of the International Waterfowl Research Bureau as the agency for international waterfowl conservation studies.

5.5.3 While bird interest has dominated the NGO scene, societies for other animal groups played their part in post-war developments. Mammals have, until recently, not presented the same kinds of conservation problems as birds, and interest has been mainly in their importance as game/sport animals or as pests. Perhaps for this reason, the Mammal Society of the British Isles has been mainly concerned with scientific studies of British mammals and the provision of technical advice. Its recently formed Bats Group has, however, become much concerned with what is now a serious conservation problem. Interest in the otter, as another declining species, has also grown mainly through the concern of animal enthusiasts amongst the NGOs. The British Herpetological Society has taken a strong lead in conservation of endangered reptiles and amphibians in terms of legislation, reserve acquisition and habitat management. The Royal Entomological Society connected its own Conservation Committee to other parties in 1968 to form a Joint Committee for the Conservation of British Insects which has promoted site conservation, species protection, codes of conduct on collecting and research interests in threatened species. Entomologists have also contributed to insect mapping schemes such as that for butterflies, which has now shown convincingly that these are one of the most threatened of all our British wildlife groups. There is now a British Butterfly Conservation Society with over 3,000 members and at least 15 local groups.

5.5.4 The British Ecological Society (BES) has continued to give the scientific leadership to research into environmental relationships of both animals and plants. After providing the impetus to the founding of the official nature conservation movement, it has maintained an academic independence, particularly in avoiding any involvement in the politics of conservation. Many BES members are nevertheless deeply concerned about and individually involved in conservation issues, and its Ecological Affairs Committee has instituted a small grants scheme for projects with strategic or applied relevance to wildlife conservation. The BES is always regarded as the leading source of expertise on vegetation and as having given the original stimulus to plant community description and mapping in Britain. Its leading figures have also pioneered studies in animal population ecology. The universities, especially through their departments of biology, botany, zoology, geology and geography, continue to give strong support to nature conservation through their research (including use of NNRs), advice and teaching, and direct participation of individual staff in extramural conservation activities is valuable. Many universities have also set up undergraduate and post-graduate courses in conservation and these have helped particularly by training people in specialist knowledge of the subject.

5.5.5 The Botanical Society of the British Isles (BSBI), with a mixed amateur and professional membership, has similarly been the leading focus for information on the status and distribution of flowering plants and ferns. The BSBI was responsible for the introduction of the system of biological mapping based on records in the 10×10 km squares of the National Grid. Its pioneering mapping scheme was launched in 1954 and led to the publication of **Atlas of the British Flora** in 1962. The method uses different symbols on the same map for different recording periods so that changes in distribution (especially declines) are immediately clear. The approach is being used to good effect in the distribution mapping of all other main groups of flora and fauna, for example in the BTO's **Atlas of Breeding Birds** and the forthcoming Butterfly Atlas. The other important feature was that the field recording was done largely by the unpaid membership guided by a full-time professional organiser. The BSBI subsequently set up a Conservation Committee to promote botanical conservation, both by site protection and through the promotion of relevant legislation. It has had a special concern with protection of rare taxa and helped to identify the list of endangered species which formed the special schedules of the 1975 and 1981 Acts. BSBI information contributed substantially to the first British Red Data Book, **Vascular Plants,** published in 1977, with a second edition in 1983.

5.5.6 Other botanical societies have become increasingly active in conservation matters. The Botanical Society of Edinburgh and the Royal Botanic Garden, Edinburgh, have promoted study of the Scottish flora. The British Lichen Society has been particularly energetic, supplying valuable information to the NC/NCC on important lichen sites and undertaking numerous surveys and also research on the adverse effects of atmospheric pollution on the British lichen flora, one of the most important in Europe. The British Bryological Society has set up a Bryophyte Conservation Committee, and the British Pteridological Society is giving attention to problems of fern conservation. Representatives of societies covering the lower plants sit on the BSBI Conservation Committee.

5.5.7 One of the most recent conservation organisations is the Woodland Trust, set up in 1972 with the objective of safeguarding our native trees and woodlands, with their associated plants and animals. The Trust already has 32,690 members and has established 111 woodland reserves by purchase or gift. It is managing these woodlands to maintain and enhance their wildlife value and is also recreating new broad-leaved woodlands. This is a valuable addition to the work of the other NGOs.

5.5.8 While geology and physiography have always had an important amateur following in the learned societies, the NC/NCC have looked especially to university earth scientists and the British Geological Survey for help in the conservation of physical features. This has been readily given and has steadily developed into a voluntary movement for geological conservation. The Geological Society of London has set up a Conservation Committee with an independent voice, and both the Geologists' Association and the Mineralogical Society take account of conservation matters. Regional museums have also become involved in the movement. These bodies have collectively played a major part in the current Geological Conservation Review, by identifying and evaluating important physical feature sites, so that the national list can be presented with confidence that it has the full backing of the earth science community and their judgement on international values.

5.5.9 Action on marine nature conservation has lagged seriously behind the rest, but interest has recently developed a strong momentum. During Underwater Conservation Year in 1977 a number of biological conservation projects were designed for divers and were continued and expanded the following year as the Underwater Conservation Programme. From this initiative developed the Underwater Conservation Society, which continued as a project-orientated group but broadened its conservation activities, becoming a member of Wildlife Link. The Society has now evolved a useful educational and advisory role and has made a valuable contribution to NCC's marine conservation research programme. As the only voluntary body in Britain with a specific commitment to the conservation of the shore and seas, it has now become the Marine Conservation Society.

5.5.10 There has similarly been a considerable growth of interest in the conservation of wildlife within the environs of town and city, reflected in the formation of a number of urban wildlife groups in the major cities. Since human populations are so largely concentrated in urban areas and it is important to cater for interest in nature close to people's homes, there is a great demand for an outlet for the growing enthusiasm for nature. The possibilities for setting up urban reserves on undeveloped or waste ground and in parks are considerable in total, and local initiatives

have produced some spectacular results. Information and experience about habitat and species management are important to the success of such developments and involve both policy and practice on introductions of plants and animals. Gardens give much scope for individual contributions to urban wildlife conservation, and even buildings have possibilities. London's natural history has long been a field of great interest and support, but the recent movement is developing much more widely and the number of promotional groups is increasing rapidly.

5.5.11 The Conservation Corps was founded by the Council for Nature in 1959 to promote practical conservation work for wildlife and amenity by young volunteers over 16 years old. Its work was consolidated in 1970 by the establishment of the British Trust for Conservation Volunteers, which now has 12 regional offices and 314 local groups. There are week-end and residential tasks on nature reserves, historic sites, amenity areas and urban land. Instruction is given in skills such as tree-planting, hedging, ditching and building stone walls, and there is a strong emphasis on training.

5.6 The broad-spectrum NGOs

5.6.1 The Council for Nature was created in 1958 mainly to act as a promotional agency for the nature conservation movement, complementing the work of the official organisation. Its role was to be especially through publicity and it was designed to win support and funds, for example by sponsoring the first National Nature Week in 1963. Three conferences on 'The Countryside in 1970' benefited greatly from the patronage of the Duke of Edinburgh. Representatives of an extremely wide range of environmental interests came together to examine the needs of conservation in relation to the competing demands of other land and resource uses in the countryside. Study groups reviewed various main issues and made recommendations for improvement: some of those on legislation were largely implemented in the Countryside Act 1968. A recommendation from the second conference that County Councils should appoint Countryside Committees soon showed positive results. The final conference examined how collective and individual efforts for conservation could be achieved. The Council of Europe also designated 1970 as European Conservation Year.

5.6.2 Within the last few years Wildlife Link has been set up as a liaison and pressure group for the whole range of nature-orientated organisations. Wildlife Link played an important part in injecting informed public opinion into the parliamentary debates on the Wildlife and Countryside Bill and in strengthening the final form of the resulting Act in 1981. The voluntary conservation movement now stands as a strong and influential lobby well able to sustain an equal partnership with the official agency, though differing in style.

5.6.3 The Council for Environmental Conservation (CoEnCo) has absorbed the responsibilities of the Council for Nature. It is concerned with wider environmental issues such as pollution, waste disposal, recreation and preservation of the built environment as well as nature conservation in the strictest sense. It produces the monthly newsletter, **habitat,** and runs an information service (partly funded by NCC) dealing with queries on environmental matters from government, the public and the media. It also produces special reports on major environmental issues and has given evidence in various formal inquiries on a variety of topics.

5.6.4 The World Wildlife Fund — United Kingdom (WWF-UK) is an important donor to wildlife conservation in the UK, and since its inception in 1961 it has given over £1·5 million directly for this purpose. In addition, it initiates and funds its own conservation programme to resolve issues in relation to the Wildlife and Countryside Act, the relationship between agricultural policy and habitat loss, badgers and bovine tuberculosis and the grey seals and fisheries problems. It also works on international issues including those involving British commercial and government activity abroad, such as the activities of the International Whaling Commission, trade in endangered species, the resources of Antarctica and EEC links. Much of this work is carried out in association with other voluntary bodies. WWF-UK was a major contributor in the funding and launching of the Conservation and Development Programme for the UK.

5.6.5 The National Trust (NT) and National Trust for Scotland (NTS) are concerned with the preservation of scenic beauty and historic buildings for public enjoyment but, while their goals are closest to those of the Countryside Commissions, their land acquisitions undoubtedly have great benefit for the protection of wildlife and physical features. The Trusts' primary objectives are regarded as fully compatible with nature conservation and this interest is given due weight in estate management plans. Many SSSIs and several NNRs are located on the Trusts' lands, and the NT has set up a Conservation Section to survey and monitor properties and advise on their management for their wildlife interest. The combined membership of the Trusts is around 1·26 million, of whom probably the majority have a keen appreciation of nature.

5.6.6 Bodies such as the Council for the Protection of Rural England, the Ramblers' Association and the Friends of the Lake District, while primarily concerned with amenity aspects of the countryside, have incidentally done much to promote the conservation of nature as well. They have acted as influential pressure groups in resisting various kinds of development damaging to the visual and recreational qualities of the countryside. The post-war period has seen the growth of other environmental groups such as Friends of the Earth (FOE) and Greenpeace, with a still wider concern for the problems and moral issues of man in relation to resources. Both are much concerned about the many forms of pollution, including especially the pervasive effects of ionising radiations from the nuclear industry, acid deposition from atmospheric discharges and the dumping of waste toxic chemicals. FOE have been especially active in publicising the scale of habitat and species loss and in campaigning for and achieving stronger legislation. Greenpeace has been responsible for much of the publicity about the international problems of whaling and sealing and about radioactive discharges and has become well known for its direct action on such issues.

5.6.7 The British Association of Nature Conservationists (BANC) was founded in 1979 to provide a forum for debate and exchange of ideas about nature conservation in its widest sense. Regular meetings focus attention on topical environmental themes, and their main proceedings are published in the journal, **Ecos,** to give a wide dissemination of the issues and views upon them. Special theme numbers have dealt with agriculture and conservation, wetlands, environmental impact assessment, the World Conservation Strategy and the politics of conservation. Other special reports on important subjects are commissioned by BANC, sometimes in conjunction with WWF and FOE.

6. The landowners, farmers and foresters

6.1 The rural community of farmers and foresters determines land-use over the larger part of this country, and their influence on nature conservation is enormous. The bodies which represent their interests and other parties with business and commercial involvement in land are also included here. The relevant official bodies are listed under 7.3 and 7.4. Agricultural interests are represented especially by the National Farmers' Union (NFU), Scottish National Farmers' Union (SNFU), Farmers' Union of Wales (FUW), Country Landowners' Association (CLA) and Scottish Landowners' Federation (SLF). Crofting, a special form of land tenure in parts of Scotland, is looked after by the official Crofters' Commission and by the Crofters' Union. Forestry and timber interests are represented by the Timber Growers' United Kingdom Ltd, the private forestry companies such as Economic Forestry Group (EFG), the Royal Forestry Society, the Royal Scottish Forestry Society and the Institute of Chartered Foresters.

6.2 Farmers and foresters regard themselves as the natural conservationists. The CLA has recently stated its view that landowners are in practice responsible for conservation. The historical role of landowners in shaping the face of rural Britain and in bestowing the legacy of wildlife and habitat as it exists today is referred to in Section 1. During the growth of the nature conservation movement over the last hundred years, farmers and foresters have certainly played a crucial part in events. The early efforts of the RSPB to protect rare birds and their eggs depended greatly on the co-operation of sympathetic landowners and farmers and their employees. The expansion of the nature reserves programme has also been facilitated by the willingness of owners to enter into leases or management agreements. Of the 195 NNRs established by the NCC, 151 are partly or wholly declared under leases or Nature Reserve Agreements with owners. Management for the nature interest often depends on continuation of previous practices.

6.3 The traditional landowners' enthusiasm for field sports is closely linked to the conservation of habitat important to wildlife on farmland. In the lowlands much of the remaining semi-natural broad-leaved woodland has survived largely because of its value as a refuge for foxes and as coverts for pheasants and woodcock. Duck-flighting ponds have created additional open water habitat, and marshy ground has been valued for its snipe-shooting. The grouse moors and deer forests in the northern hill country also tend to be more important as wildlife areas than uplands managed wholly for sheep or the conifer forests which are now increasingly replacing them. Bodies representing the field sports interest, such as the Game Conservancy, British Field Sports Society, British Association for Shooting and Conservation (the former WAGBI) and the British Falconers' Club have contributed in their various ways to nature conservation.

6.4 Angling has long been an important factor in the conservation of lakes and rivers, both lowland and upland. Game fishing is a valuable source of income on some estates, and coarse fishing has become an enormously popular pastime appealing to many city dwellers. Fishing interests are represented by the Salmon and Trout Association, the Anglers' Co-operative Association, the Sea Anglers' Association and the Standing Committee on Countryside Sports. Conservation of commercial fish is the responsibility of the Ministry of Agriculture, Fisheries and Food and the Department of Agriculture and Fisheries for Scotland.

6.5 Many farmers, foresters and fishermen are keen naturalists, and their numbers have increased as part of the growth of the conservation movement. From their own interest they wish to look after the wild plants and animals on their land. Most others also feel a particular pride in knowing that they have something special, such as a wildlife rarity, on their ground and will take particular care to cherish this. Many owners and occupiers have established private nature reserves and taken special measures to conserve their wildlife.

6.6 This is the positive side of the story, but there is, unfortunately, a negative side, and this goes to the very heart of the present nature conservation problem. The truth is that, however much we owe to landowners and occupiers from the past and however laudable their positive efforts at present may be, recent economic forces and government policy for agriculture have led to practices highly inimical to the conservation of nature. Farmers, seeing themselves as the real practitioners of conservation and custodians of the countryside, are upset to find a wave of criticism levelled at their activities by nature conservationists. The problems are largely to do with the incompatibility of the needs of maximum production and of wildlife management, but they are then compounded by a confusion over the meaning of the term nature conservation. To a farmer, nature is his farm, and the idea of conserving it is inseparable from that of good and efficient management of the farm. What is so often overlooked is that good farm management today is vastly different in its environmental effects from good management only a couple of generations ago. Many landowners are troubled at the trend of events, but many others seem to be puzzled at the apparent contradiction. Some recognise the issue but say that farming comes first.

6.7 Even for those farmers with a strong personal interest in wildlife, the freedom to practice nature conservation (in the naturalists' sense) is thus strictly constrained by the economic necessity of using modern farming techniques. Many have refrained of their own choice from operations harmful to wildlife and its habitat, or have modified developments beneficially, while some have deliberately managed or recreated habitat to improve its wildlife value. The recent support for the FWAG movement is also an important indication of farmers' greatly increased interest in wildlife. These efforts are appreciated, but even in total they are small when set against the overwhelmingly adverse impact of modern agriculture on wildlife and its habitat in Britain since 1940. The character of this impact is dealt with again later under 12.2 and 14.3.

6.8 Forestry too has a long and proud tradition of conservation, explicitly recognised in the office of Conservator in the Forestry Commission. Foresters have thus also been disconcerted to find that their own evaluation of the benefits of their recent activities to wildlife conservation has not always been accepted by the conservationists themselves. Modern forestry practice is very different from the silvicultural methods which maintained our woodlands as the richest type of wildlife habitat in this country, and it shows some parallels with the trends and effects of high technology farming. The same semantic and conceptual confusion has therefore arisen over the meaning of the word conservation. The objective of maximising the crop yield in existing woodlands creates a degree of incompatibility

with wildlife management. It is true that many commercial forests, both long-established and recent, have considerable wildlife value and that they are nearly always a better option than intensive agriculture; but they are highly variable in this respect and taken as a whole are much less valuable than ancient semi-natural woodland. It is no doubt true also that the extensive new conifer forests offer great opportunities for wildlife conservation, but the issue is complex and the crucial question is how far this potential will ever be realised (see also 15.9.12). Amenity tree-planting programmes are helping to restore the losses of hedgerow trees, and are welcome, but they are of greater benefit to landscape than to wildlife.

6.9 As the problems of competition between land-use development and nature conservation have grown, the users' organisations have increasingly become involved as mediators. The NFU, CLA and SLF in particular have tried to persuade both sides in disputes to see the other's case and to reach better understanding. The users' organisations have done much to convey the nature conservation message to their members and to seek accommodation with the wildlife side over conflicts.

6.10 This coming together of the different interests is exemplified by the Farming and Wildlife Advisory Group and its expansion from a National Committee to County Committees, some with full-time professional advisers. There is general optimism that this bringing together of representatives of government agricultural agencies, farming and land-using organisations, farmers themselves and nature conservationists will be a beneficial way of tackling issues in the countryside. The nature conservation bodies welcome the development of FWAGs as an important means of inducing the agricultural community itself to seek resolution of problems and to develop further its interest in wildlife.

The role of other public bodies

7.1 **The Department of the Environment**
7.1.1 The Department of the Environment (DoE) has acted as the sponsoring department for the reconstituted Nature Conservancy Council since 1973. NCC is an independent council with direct access to the Secretary of State, but receives its funds through DoE and is responsible to that Department for financial, establishments and other administrative procedures. In giving advice to Ministers it also normally operates through the Directorate of Rural Affairs (DRA), which has overall responsibility for countryside matters, including nature conservation, scenic amenity and recreation, common land, planning, socio-economic and environmental issues and related legislation. DoE has an extremely broad remit in regard to land-use policy and seeks to integrate different sectional interests in advising Ministers.

7.1.2 In Scotland, the functions of DoE reside with the Scottish Office in the Scottish Development Department (SDD), and the Secretary of State for Scotland has an overview on all matters of environmental concern to government. An important strategic input to site safeguard in Scotland was made in 1977 through the National Planning Guidelines for Large Industrial Sites and Rural Conservation prepared by SDD. Similarly, in Wales environmental affairs are dealt with by the Welsh Office and Secretary of State for Wales. NCC in Scotland and Wales thus relates to central government through these channels. DoE also represents the UK on many international conservation matters.

7.2 **The Countryside Commissions**
7.2.1 The two official agencies whose functions are closest to the nature conservation movement are the Countryside Commission (CC), with status parallel to NCC as an independent council within the DoE ambit, and the Countryside Commission for Scotland (CCS), reporting to the Scottish office. These bodies are responsible for promoting the conservation and enhancement of the natural beauty and scenic amenity of the countryside and encouraging its enjoyment by the public as a recreational asset. These objectives are achieved through giving advice and grant-aid to local authorities and voluntary bodies for a variety of conservation tasks including land acquisition, tree-planting, Country Parks, picnic sites, wardening and information. In England and Wales the CC designates National Parks and Areas of Outstanding Natural Beauty and defines Heritage Coasts; it also advises on their administration and the development of facilities for information and interpretation. The CCS has felt that the objectives of National Parks could be achieved in other ways and has designated 40 National Scenic Areas, within which natural beauty is conserved through planning measures and management agreements.

7.2.2 Other activities of these bodies include designating long-distance footpaths, studying and advising on major countryside issues (e.g. the landscape problems caused by modern agriculture), urban fringe projects, setting up demonstration farms and sponsoring research and experimental work with a strong practical bias related to conservation and recreational problems. Such work, and also the development of Country Parks, has given a strong lead in creative conservation (see 15.9). There is also the important function of disseminating knowledge and giving advice and information through publications, conferences and other public relations work, including promoting the Country Code.

7.2.3 The interests and activities of these countryside agencies thus run in close parallel to those of the nature conservation bodies, though they differ in their greater emphasis on wildlife (especially vegetation) and physical features as determinants of landscape, and thus on their visual qualities and recreational use. The CC and CCS have made a large contribution to nature conservation in the special sense, by restricting adverse development through planning control and through their promotional activities listed above.

7.3 **The agriculture departments**
7.3.1 From the beginning, the NC developed liaison and consultation with the Ministry of Agriculture, Fisheries and Food (MAFF) and the Department of Agriculture for Scotland (DAFS), and later with the Welsh Office Agriculture Department (WOAD). These departments express government policy on agriculture and thus

largely determine land-use over at least 80% of Britain's surface (Figure 3). They accordingly exert enormous influence on nature, although their direct responsibility for managing land is very limited. Agricultural policy since the Agriculture Act 1947 has been directed especially to the efficient production of cheap food, maintenance of income and living standards for farmers and workers, and adequacy of return on capital investment. It has aimed to maximise domestic food production by using modern farming technology supported by public subsidy in various forms (**Food from our own Resources,** Cmnd 6020). Departmental interest in wild flora and fauna has been largely from the viewpoint of pests and damage to crops, animals and foodstuffs.

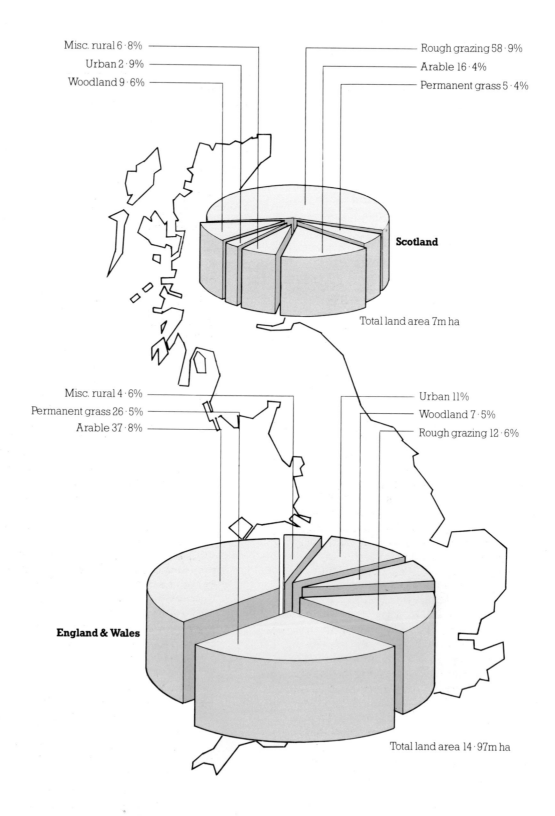

Misc. rural 6·8%
Urban 2·9%
Woodland 9·6%

Rough grazing 58·9%
Arable 16·4%
Permanent grass 5·4%

Scotland

Total land area 7m ha

Misc. rural 4·6%
Permanent grass 26·5%
Arable 37·8%

Urban 11%
Woodland 7·5%
Rough grazing 12·6%

England & Wales

Total land area 14·97m ha

Figure 3: Pattern of land use in England, Wales and Scotland

	England (hectares)	Wales (hectares)	Scotland (hectares)
1 Arable land	5,278,186	263,397	1,125,868
2 All grass (5 years old and over)	3,170,596	845,031	562,647
3 Rough grazing	1,189,172	531,428	4,272,566
4 Woodland	175,945	31,654	65,711
5 All other agricultural land	136,352	13,022	35,517
6 Inland waters	72,779	12,950	160,321
7 Urban area (1971 est.)	——— 1,650,000 ———		225,000
8 Broadleaved woodlands (productive)	459,000	61,000	76,000
9 Coniferous high forest (productive)	395,000	172,000	831,000
10 Unproductive woodland (scrub and felled woodland)	91,000	10,000	71,000

Figures at 1-5 are taken from **Agricultural statistics: UK; 1982:** figures at 6 from **Whitaker's Almanack;**
figures at 7 from **The Planner,** January 1976; figures at 8-10 from the FC's **Forestry facts and figures 1982-83;**

The Countryside Act 1968, however, required departments representing land and resource users to "have regard to the desirability of conserving the natural beauty [including flora, fauna and geological features] and amenity of the countryside" in the pursuance of their interests. MAFF promotes land drainage and flood alleviation schemes through substantial grants to Water Authorities and Internal Drainage Boards. Since 1981 MAFF has been required to exercise its duties with regard to these bodies so as to further the conservation and enhancement of natural beauty and the conservation of flora, fauna and geological and physiographic features of special interest.

7.3.2 The promotion of governmental agricultural policy has been in the forefront of the heated public debate on the losses of wildlife and habitat attributable to farming in recent years. This issue is discussed later (14.3.3), but the agriculture departments have found little scope within their statutory remit for directly assisting nature conservation, except through their discretion over grant-aid for farm operations which would adversely affect nature conservation interests. When they decline grant-aid on these grounds on an SSSI, NCC is legally required to provide compensation for development profit forgone. Numerous commentators have, however, pointed out that grant-aid is only a small part of the issue and that the main problems of agricultural policy for wildlife stem from the much more massive indirect public subsidies which underwrite the whole food pricing, market manipulation and farmer income system, especially in relation to the EEC's Common Agricultural Policy. Within the scope allowed, the Agricultural Development and Advisory Service (ADAS) and its equivalents in the Scottish Agricultural Colleges have been helpful in promoting an interest in nature conservation amongst farmers and in giving appropriate management advice. NCC has developed a close and beneficial relationship with ADAS over the Wildlife and Countryside Act, and ADAS is closely involved in the work of FWAG.

7.4

The Forestry Commission

7.4.1 The Forestry Commission (FC) is the state forest authority and the forest enterprise, charged with the conduct of government forestry policy. It has increasingly affirmed its intention to promote nature conservation within its own forest estate, in so far as this is compatible with its primary objective of the efficient production of wood for industry. The FC recognises the importance of its forests for wildlife — both the broad-leaved lowland types and the much more extensive new upland woods, mainly of conifers. It aims to safeguard these woods as wildlife habitats, and where practicable to improve them, and also to give particular attention to those sites where nature conservation has been identified as specially important. Management pays particular attention to the wildlife value of plantation edges, existing broad-leaved trees and scrub, dead trees, open water, rocky habitats, glades, rides and roadsides. Several Forest Nature Reserves have been set up, and the Commission has leased a number of areas to the nature conservation bodies to establish reserves. The wide development of public recreational facilities within the state forests includes nature trails and wildlife exhibits in information and interpretative centres. Forest rangers are often wildlife experts and do a good deal of management and bird protection work, as well as contributing observations to survey, recording and other research. The Commission also looks to the conservation bodies for advice.

7.4.2 The FC also supports private sector forestry with grant-aid, advice and other help. Its role here is analogous to that of ADAS, and similar issues arise over the Commission's discretion to withhold grant-aid for forestry operations because of their damaging effects on wildlife of the areas concerned, but again NCC is responsible for finding compensation for profit forgone.

7.5   Other departments and public utilities
7.5.1 Of the other departments with a particular concern for land and natural resources, the Ministry of Defence (MoD) has been especially responsive, appointing a Conservation Officer and showing considerable interest in the appropriate management of its training areas. Some of these have been havens for wildlife, not least because they have kept other developments at bay. Others, such as St Kilda, would be less well cared for as reserves and SSSIs without the presence of MoD. Porton Down in Wiltshire and the Stanford Practical Training Area in the Breckland have become two of the most important wildlife areas now left in lowland England. Within the constraints of its primary purpose, MoD issues access permits to naturalists and fosters recreational interest in wildlife by services personnel.

7.5.2 Departments and agencies concerned with urban, industrial, transport and energy developments all impinge on the interests of the nature conservation movement, and consultation is normally channelled through NCC. An emergency procedure for dealing with oil spills around the coast is operated by the Department of Transport's Marine Pollution Control Unit with advice from the NCC, in liaison with the RSPB and animal protection societies. The NCC advises the Department of Energy over the exploitation of existing energy sources and the development of new ones, such as tidal barrages, wave and wind power. The Department of Energy has been particularly helpful in instituting procedures to minimise environmental drainage from offshore oil exploration and production. The NCC consults with the National Coal Board over the impact of mining and land restoration. The CEGB and other public bodies involved in electricity production have been concerned to take account of nature conservation and consult the NCC over the selection of sites for new power stations; nevertheless their activities have a significant impact, not least through atmospheric pollution. The CEGB has set up nature trails and field study facilities on non-operational land. British Rail have recognised the nature conservation importance of their embankments, cut-

tings and disused railway lines, several areas of which have been sold as nature reserves. The British Waterways Board is responsible for the major part of the canal network and its feeder reservoirs and the NCC advises it on the management of 41 SSSIs. NCC and the NGOs are usually in the position of making representations to these bodies to reduce the damaging effects of their activities. The same applies over new road construction, the Department of Transport recognises the importance of motorway and road verges to wildlife and has been helpful in facilitating their study and over their actual management. The Crown Estate Commissioners own areas, especially foreshore, with high nature conservation value, and some of this lies within NNRs and SSSIs.

7.6   Water Authorities
7.6.1 While DoE and SDD have central responsibility for water and sewage policy the job of water supply and quality control for industrial and domestic users is delegated to the regional Water Authorities in England and Wales and local River Purification Boards and local authorities in Scotland. Land drainage and flood alleviation are carried out by regional Water Authorities and Internal Drainage Boards with grant aid from MAFF; in Scotland these works are the responsibility of SDD, DAFS and local authorities. The NCC has established liaison arrangements with the River Purification Boards and consultation with regional Water Authorities together with the Countryside Commissions, RSPB, RSNC and local Trusts. This consultation, together with the strengthening of Water Authorities' conservation duties, has helped to avoid damage to wildlife habitats.

7.6.2 The creation of water supply reservoirs can have damaging effects on nature conservation interests by partly or wholly drowning important sites, but there are often gains, especially in bird life, and some lowland reservoirs in agricultural settings have become nationally important sites for waterfowl. In these instances, Water Authorities have been helpful in establishing reserve areas, as at the large new lakes of Grafham and Rutland Waters. River flow management has probably given rise to larger conservation problems, but the conservation bodies have provided advice to river engineers on ways of minimising damage to wildlife during necessary operations, and some Water Authorities have responded well and particularly tried to avoid damage to river SSSIs. Greater restriction over use of herbicides to control aquatic vegetation has also been achieved. Concern for water quality has led to general reduction in river pollution, and Water Authority biologists have taken greater account of the specific wildlife criteria for water quality. Considerable improvements have been achieved in river water quality and it is hoped that discharge consents under the recently implemented Control of Pollution Acts will reflect the requirements of aquatic flora and fauna.

7.7 **The Natural Environment Research Council**

7.7.1 When the former NC was removed in 1973 (see 4.1), NERC lost responsibility for nature conservation policy and practice. Support for nature conservation research nevertheless still remains part of the NERC Charter, and work in this field is an integral part in the fulfilment of the Council's role as a source of impartial scientific advice and knowledge on the environment. In addition to applied research commissions from NCC, most of the strategic and basic research underpinning the practice of nature conservation is still being carried out by NERC, mainly on Science Budget funds. The Institute of Terrestrial Ecology, the Freshwater Biological Association and the marine laboratories are especially concerned with such studies and have even increased work on development and evaluation of survey methodology. NERC are responsible for research and advice on conservation of seals, and have a Sea Mammal Research Unit for this purpose. NERC also funds a substantial amount of fundamental conservation research in the universities. In geological matters, NERC's British Geological Survey provides NCC with advice on important sites, such as irreplaceable landforms, key stratigraphic exposures and proposed geological SSSIs, and has alerted NCC to activities threatening such sites. While regarding objectivity as essential to their research, many NERC staff are also personally committed to nature conservation.

7.8 **Local authorities**

7.8.1 Local government has played an increasing part within the nature conservation movement, in a wide variety of ways. One of the most important has been the role of planning, which has allowed NCC and the NGOs to make inputs to Structure, Local and Subject Plans in regard both to special sites and to more general conservation objectives. While not all determinations of planning applications on SSSIs have been favourable to the conservation side, there has been growing sympathy for their protection. Local authorities vary greatly in their attitudes to nature conservation, but some of the most concerned have already developed local nature conservation strategies which safeguard significant wildlife areas, promote public interest through education

and develop leisure-time enjoyment of nature. In developing environmental policies, many local authorities have employed ecologists (at least 60) who work across the range of departments, infusing ecological and conservation thinking wherever possible. The Metropolitan County Councils have pioneered the way in urban conservation, and there is now widespread enthusiasm for this activity as a means of recreation and education. Rehabilitation of waste land, including the creation of new landscapes and habitats, has been important in some areas, within a range of urban fringe projects.

7.8.2 Other important measures are the setting-up and management of Local Nature Reserves (105 in 1983) and management of Country Parks with wildlife conservation as a major objective. Heritage Coast projects have also been developed. Tree-planting, woodland and roadside verge management have been widely supported, either directly or through grants and advice, as part of general countryside support schemes. There has been significant support in money, materials and expertise to such bodies as Nature Conservation Trusts, FWAGs, Environmental Records Centres, the Woodland Trust and local wildlife groups. Public awareness has also been encouraged through interpretative centres, guided walks and farm open days. Local authorities have also promoted major surveys and collection and co-ordination of information relating wildlife, both independently and in co-operation with the conservation bodies. In the development of countryside policies there is growing recognition of the heritage concept of nature and provision for its conservation. There is also increasing support for environmental education, both in schools and other institutions and through public facilities such as museums.

7.9 **National Park authorities**

7.9.1 The ten National Parks, covering 9% of England and Wales, are all in upland country of the west and the north, and contain many areas of the highest importance to nature conservation. The administering Park authorities are responsible for protecting the landscape and wildlife features whilst providing for informal public recreation. They operate through planning and development control, land management, ranger services, and environmental educational and interpretative services for visitors. The Parks make a considerable contribution towards habitat and species protection and work closely with the nature conservation organisations. Many of their staff are ecologists, natural scientists and committed conservationists, and wardens often become involved in wildlife protection. The Park authorities have taken particular action to conserve broad-leaved woodlands and moorland by acquiring considerable areas of these habitats, by securing voluntary restraints on adverse land-use developments, by management agreements over vulnerable areas and through the consultations which farmers are required to make over intended developments grant-aided by MAFF. Commercial afforestation is not subject to statutory control but is subject to consultation and has been restricted through agreements in some Parks.

8

Industry

8.1 Industrial development tends to affect nature adversely both by directly taking land within areas of wildlife or geological interest and by producing environmental pollution through its waste products. In recognition of its responsibility, the oil industry has, during the development of the North Sea oilfields, taken measures to minimise the risks to seabirds through prevention of offshore oil spills. Some of the major oil companies have provided funds for surveys of seabirds, both for nesting colonies and at sea. Abandoned mineral workings, especially flooded sand, gravel and clay excavations but also quarries can develop into valuable wildlife habitats. Mineral companies, particularly those dealing with aggregates, have co-operated with conservation interests in managing some disused sites beneficially for wildlife, including creation of nature reserves. The chemical industry, especially that part producing pesticides, has been associated with wildlife problems. Measures to reduce or eliminate the use of the most problematical pesticides and industrial pollutants, notably the persistent organochlorine compounds, have greatly alleviated the earlier hazards to birds and other animals. Manufacturers' co-operation through the Pesticides Safety Precautions Scheme over the screening of new chemicals has helped to minimise further problems. Constant vigilance is nevertheless needed over toxic chemicals in the environment. Additionally, commercial sponsorship of nature conservation is a new field for development and recent projects include the donation of a nature reserve and the production of booklets and educational guides.

9

Education, the media and recreation

9.1 Finally, there are the activities and organisations which contribute to public awareness and interest in the subject, beyond the work of the conservation bodies themselves. This begins with school education, in which the teaching of environmental studies, biology and ecology has increased greatly since 1950 and created a parallel need for areas suitable for fieldwork. Higher education has expanded the treatment of environmental and conservation issues, notably in university courses, and the subject now appears in some agricultural and forestry degree curricula. Spare-time courses and evening classes in kindred subjects have multiplied, and the Field Studies Council and the Field Studies Association, with their educational Field Centres, have risen in prominence. A Council for Environmental Education and the Scottish Environmental Education Committee have been created and have an active promotional role over the whole field, as has the National Association for Environmental Education (formerly Rural Studies Association).

9.2 Other learned and educational institutions have become involved with nature conservation. The Royal Botanic Garden at Kew has taken a lead in international plant conservation through its influence in guiding and implementing the law on trade in endangered flora and in forming a seed bank and propagating material in cultivation. Other botanic gardens are contributing to propagation of rare and endangered British plants through support from NCC. Zoological gardens, including private collections, have an important educational value and some are providing a means of last resort for saving certain globally rare animals from extinction by breeding them in captivity — in some cases for restocking in the wild. The museums, including the British Museum (Natural History), have developed conservation and ecological exhibits and have an important role in stimulating interest in natural history, especially amongst the young. Some provincial museums and universities have developed local records centres supplementing the national collection of data in the Biological Records Centre of ITE. Their collections also continue to be an important source of reference and data supporting survey and other research.

The Royal Society of Edinburgh has a continuing programme of symposia and publications on the natural environment.

9.3 The post-war development of the conservation movement has involved a growth industry in literature, art and the media for public information. The number and quality of books, magazines and journals on natural history have grown enormously. Photography, including the refinement of the 35mm camera and colour film, has made enormous strides, and nature subjects are an important factor in its commercial importance both in illustrating publications and as a personal hobby. Nature illustrators, especially bird painters, have grown in numbers, and the demand for their work is endless. Wildlife films have a great popularity which owes much to the development of this medium by the RSPB, the BBC Natural History Unit, Anglia Television and other commercial television producers. Press coverage of conservation issues has increased greatly, and some newspaper correspondents have developed a special interest in this field. Package holidays and tours with a wildlife emphasis have become popular both at home and abroad. Some other recreational interests have become involved in conservation, such as the British Sub-Aqua Club, which has helped with marine surveys. Nature is now a recreational and tourist asset of the greatest importance.

Part II
The present position and future prospects

10

Analysis of achievements

10.1 Objectives for nature conservation have been rather loosely and qualitatively set in the past, so that measures of attainment or shortfall are not easily made. While the 1949 NC Charter did not set any quantitative targets for the three main functions, Cmd 7122 nevertheless made quite specific recommendations, with its lists of proposed nature reserves and other protected area categories. For the wider countryside no targets for conservation achievement were even discussed. It was generally assumed that the NC would do what was feasible and should be satisfied if species' populations could be maintained somewhere between the extremes of explosion and extinction and if habitat loss could be contained within reasonable limits. Although the SPNR had its own list of prospective nature reserves, the voluntary movement as a whole had imprecise targets.

10.2 The most obvious yardstick of attainments would be to assess how much of the resource of nature is left, and how much has been lost, since conservation programmes began. This is no easy task since earlier base-line measurements of the resource are so sketchy. The setting of a base-line in time is arbitrary also, though 1950 would seem an appropriate date. In general, too, conservation successes amount to no more than maintaining the *status quo*. There are few opportunities for actually increasing or enhancing the resource of nature and the victories are usually the prevention of further loss. In this sense, conservation is a largely defensive process, reducing the scale of human impact and contrasting with other land-use activities such as agriculture, which are positive through continuous development and expansion of their products. The positive avenues for nature conservation are largely through management activities, notably the re-creation or restoration of lost or damaged habitats and the reintroduction or restocking of vanished or declining species. Only a few modern man-made habitats incidentally provide important wildlife opportunities, for example reservoirs for wintering birds and flooded gravel pits for aquatic life generally.

10.3 Even when conservation gains and losses are measurable, or at least identifiable, their significance as successes or failures must inevitably be a matter for subjective judgement. Views on some issues also vary widely according to standpoint. And it is seldom that any particular issue can be regarded wholly as a success or a failure, so that qualifications of such judgements are usually necessary.

Successes

11.1 Nature reserves and Sites of Special Scientific Interest

11.1.1 The most solid and measurable achievement has been the actual tally of protected areas. Figure 1 summarises the nature reserve holdings of NCC and the NGOs and shows how far the proposals in Cmd 7122, Cmd 7814 and the later NCR have been met. The number and extent of important areas now specifically protected for their nature conservation interest provide a valuable hard core to the total effort. Within these areas are some of the best examples in Britain of natural or semi-natural vegetation with their distinctive animal communities, some of the largest populations of local or rare species, some of the most endangered species, and some of the most important geological and physiographic features. Figure 1 also summarises the numbers and areas of SSSIs.

11.2 Conservation by persuasion

11.2.1 The approach through persuasion is more difficult to measure and, despite many successes, it must also admit to numerous shortfalls, if not outright failures. One of the biggest successes has been the winning of the battle over the adverse effects of certain pesticides on wildlife. The evidence from research into the problem by the conservation bodies was powerful enough to obtain progressive withdrawal of the most damaging compounds, and beneficial effects were shown within a few years by incipient recovery of the affected raptor species. These have continued to the point where the conservation problem of the organochlorine insecticides is much diminished. Parallel approaches to other forms of chemical pollution, particularly in many rivers and in the sea, have also brought about reduction in hazards to wildlife.

11.2.2 Such problems are international, and nature conservationists' anxiety over toxic chemical problems was in the forefront of the great wave of environmental concern which has spread around the world since 1960. The NC was in the vanguard of the movement through

Deeping Lakes SSSI, Lincolnshire

its work on new synthetic herbicides in the early 1950s and its anticipatory attempts to convince government of the potential seriousness of the pesticide issue as the danger signals appeared. The rapid response of the BTO and RSPB to evidence of bird 'kills' by toxic seed dressings in the late 1950s showed the value of an early warning system for identifying field problems through the efforts of a network of voluntary observers. The need for both predictive ability and monitoring programmes as part of a detection system for environmental problems is now an understood part of conservation strategy. The lessons have been applied to other issues. Nevertheless, the problem of oil pollution at sea clearly shows that with some environmental hazards an ineradicable element of human error or misdemeanour can produce sudden disaster, and the threat of a catastrophic incident remains ever present.

11.2.3 In general, the nature conservation movement has succeeded in raising the level of public awareness of the main issues and in informing people about problems and desirable solutions. The actual response has been somewhat variable; there are few if any areas in which beneficial result has been totally lacking, but the return in positive action has sometimes been weak or ineffective. Nevertheless, a trend of improvement has been established, and within the main land and natural resource user groups there has been increased willingness to consider the needs of nature conservation in the pursuit of primary objectives. The concern to make contributions or at least concessions to nature conservation is shown in numerous ways within Sections 6, 7 and 8. It is evident in the greater responsiveness of government departments and agencies, public utilities, local authorities, relevant parts of industry and business, landowners and occupiers and their organisations. The recognition now given to nature conservation inputs to planning at various levels, the concern shown by other resource use interests to pay regard to its need, and the much increased liaison and consultation with these interests must all be regarded as substantial gains within the last 35 years. The reception of the FWAG system exemplifies the trend and is encouraging.

11.3   Legislation
11.3.1 Government recognition of nature conservation is reflected in new legislation which enhanced the strength of the 1949 Act — first the Protection of Birds Act 1954 (updated in 1967) and the Countryside Acts of 1967 and 1968, which made it a statutory requirement for other land and natural resource users represented within government to have regard to nature conservation. In 1975 the Conservation of Wild Creatures and Wild Plants Act extended special protection to certain rare animals and vascular plants and forbade the uprooting of any wild plants without permission. These improvements culminated in 1981 in the Wildlife and Countryside Act, with its new powers (see 4.4). Most conservationists regard the provisions for SSSIs as the most significant new measure, representing a major shift in ability to safeguard important areas. The devices now available, including the Nature Conservation Order, are strengthened, though their price has been the adoption of the principle of compensation for development profit forgone and their effectiveness will depend primarily on continuing government willingness to meet the cost.

11.3.2 The law protecting flora and fauna has more effect with some species or groups than others. For birds, it has greatly curtailed indiscriminate killing and taking for sport and food, but it has been far less effective in stopping the killing of alleged predators of game or stock, the taking of birds (especially raptors) to keep in captivity and the collecting of eggs as a hobby. Such shortcomings are, however, mainly a reflection of difficulties in enforcement. It is too early yet to assess the value of wild plant protection. The wildlife protection laws help also to generate a climate of opinion which accepts the importance of and responsibility for wildlife.

11.3.3 The British conservation movement has contributed significantly to the development and implementation of various international measures for wildlife habitat and species protection. Both the bodies and the legislation mentioned in 3.10 and 15.7 have greatly advanced nature conservation overseas and have had beneficial influence in Britain also.

11.4   Birds
11.4.1 The story of bird conservation is, on the whole, one of the successes. Despite some serious long-term declines in population, many species have either maintained their numbers remarkably well or actually increased. And many more species now breed in Britain than were known at the turn of the century. The situation is a tribute to the effectiveness of the enormous effort which has gone into bird conservation, especially the protection and public education aspects, but it reflects achievements under all the previous three headings (11.1-11.3). The great increase in new afforestation has had beneficial effects on the numbers and

Top left: Mountain avens

Top right: Wartbiter grasshopper

Centre left: Bee eater

Centre right: Great crested newt

Bottom left: Barn owl

Right: Whooper swan

Bottom right: Sheep's-bit and thrift

45

distribution of some species, but the balance sheet of changes also has a debit side (Figure 4). And for some habitats, bird conservation cannot be regarded as a success.

11.5 Geological and physiographic conservation

11.5.1 The protection of physical features has been one of the most successful activities: very few important sites (apart from limestone pavements) have been destroyed, and the Geology and Physiography Section of NC/NCC has had only two unfavourable verdicts in a large number of public inquiries. Beyond this, the growth of concern and involvement amongst the community of earth scientists has been largely the result of the Section's efforts in promoting a scientific service and receiving reciprocal support from the 'users'.

11.6 Growth of the nature conservation movement

11.6.1 Arguably, the most striking achievement of the nature conservation movement since 1950 has been its own growth, most spectacularly shown by the increase in the actual number and membership of the voluntary

organisations (see Section 5). It has been estimated that at least one million people in Britain have a substantial interest in wildlife, and a much larger number derive enjoyment from contact with nature. The popularity of television and radio nature programmes, press coverage and the large output of books and periodicals about wildlife and the countryside are further evidence of the considerable public enthusiasm for nature and the wider awareness of conservation issues.

Vallis Vale

Holyhead Coast

Figure 4: Post-1950 decline in breeding bird populations in Britain

Farmland habitats (F) (including trees/small woods and uncultivated grassland)	Reason for decline
Corncrake	Modernisation of agriculture, especially mechanised hay/cereal cutting.
Grey partridge	Modernisation of agriculture, reduction of habitat variety.
Rook (W)	Extensive conversion of grassland to arable.
Corn bunting	Uncertain: belongs almost wholly to farmland.
Yellowhammer (H)	Modernisation of agriculture, reduction of habitat variety.
Cirl bunting (H)	Ploughing of old grassland, removal of hedges and scrub.
Tree pipit (H)	Ploughing of old grassland, removal of scrub and woodland.
Cuckoo (H, U)	Modernisation of agriculture, reduction of habitat variety.
Yellow wagtail	Draining and improvement of wet meadowland.
Common snipe (U, Wet)	Draining and improvement of wet meadowland.
Redshank (Wet, U)	Draining and improvement of wet meadowland.
Lapwing (D, U, Wet)	Ploughing or improvement of grassland.
Barn owl (W)	Modernisation of agriculture, reduction of habitat variety.
Little owl (W)	Modernisation of agriculture, reduction of habitat variety.
Long-eared owl (W)	Uncertain.
Sparrowhawk (W)	Organochlorine pesticides and reduction of habitat variety.
Kestrel (H, U)	Organochlorine pesticides and reduction of habitat variety.
Wryneck	Uncertain.

Heathland, partly wooded or scrub grown, including young forest (H)

Nightjar (W)	Other unknown factors.	
Red-backed shrike (F)	Possibly climatic change.	Reclamation for agriculture, invasion by woodland, post-myxomatosis changes in vegetation, and heath fires.
Woodlark (D)	Also hard winters.	
Dartford warbler	Gorse burning, also hard winters.	
Whinchat (U)		
Stonechat (U, C)		

Open downland and short grass-heath (D)

Stone curlew Wheatear (U)	Reclamation for agriculture and post-myxomatosis vegetation changes.
Chough (U-Wales)	Same, but on coastal grass-heaths.

Woodland (W)

Nightingale	Wood removal, replanting with conifers, cessation of coppicing.

Wetlands (Wet)

Water rail	Reclamation of lowland marshes and fens.
Bittern	Die-back of reed beds.
Marsh warbler	Reclamation of lowland marshes and reduction in osier-growing.
Montagu's harrier (H, U)	Uncertain, pesticides a strong possibility.
Marsh harrier	Uncertain, pesticides a strong possibility.
Kingfisher	Organochlorine insecticides, hard winters and grading of river banks.

Upland grasslands, heaths and blanket bogs (U)

Raven (C)	Afforestation, reclamation and improved sheep husbandry.
Dunlin (C)	Afforestation and draining of bogs.
Golden plover	Afforestation, reclamation.
Curlew (F)	Afforestation, reclamation.
Red grouse	Afforestation, reclamation, regression of heather moor under heavy grazing and burning, organochlorine pesticides implicated in winter range.
Merlin	

Coastlands (C)

Little tern	Disturbance to shingle beach nesting habitats.

Occurrence in other habitats is indicated in brackets. (For key see main headings).

Many other bird species have declined at least locally, but some of these have also increased in other places. The above list is restricted to those species which have shown long-term decline over at least a major part of their range, and seem to have little prospect of recovering to their pre-1950 population levels because the loss of their habitats has been too extensive.

11.6.2 Public demand and support for nature conservation are thus at an unprecedentedly high level and the upward trend is likely to continue. The position was well reflected in the parliamentary and public debates on the Wildlife and Countryside Bill, which proved to be a much more complex, time-consuming and controversial piece of legislation than had seemed likely. Nature conservation is now regarded as a major area of public interest in land and natural resource use and has thus come to have political clout.

11.7   **Research achievements**
11.7.1 Research has been especially the province of NC/NCC and NERC, through internal effort, contracts and grant-aid. The total research support involved has made a significant contribution to the post-war development of ecology as a science and to the training of ecologists. Some major 'in-house' scientific achievements resulted from themes mentioned under 3.8, and a great deal of successful management research on habitats and species has been conducted. A vast amount of work was supported in the universities, over a wide spectrum of the life and earth sciences, and a large number of publications has resulted.

11.8   **International acclaim**
11.8.1 Finally, Britain has not only made a substantial contribution to nature conservation overseas in various ways, but has also won the esteem of the international conservation community. This country is now a world leader in conservation technology, and its work on site evaluation and safeguard, reserve management, pesticides and wildlife issues, bird protection and public relations is held in high regard by other nations.

Failures

12.1 The integrated concept of conservation

12.1.1 To some people, the most serious and disappointing shortcoming in nature conservation practice has been the failure to translate into reality the broad and integrated concept of conservation which was the great vision of Cmd 7122. The reasons are various, but chief among them was an under-estimation of the political implications, stemming especially from the existence of powerful entrenched interests within the larger field of conservation originally conceived. Other land-use interests, such as agriculture and forestry, did not welcome the involvement of the NC in their affairs. The implications for interference in, or adjudication over, policy of these other interests tended to be regarded as territorial intrusions within other organisations' concerns. Increasingly, too, it has become clear that the aims of other land- and resource-use interests are nowadays often incompatible and therefore in competition with those of nature protection (see 14.3). This helps to explain why there has been considerable recent resistance to the concept of a national land-use strategy, or indeed to any proposals which could be interpreted as involving a significant change to the *status quo* in control of land-use.

12.1.2 Another impediment to the NC/NCC's scope for developing the integrated concept of conservation is that there is only a handful of native species in Britain, apart from soil organisms and perhaps pollinating insects, with significant direct economic value, that is to say deer, rabbits, game birds, wildfowl and a few tree species. The native game fish of fresh water and the marine fish with commercial value have always been regarded as the concern of the fisheries departments. The importance of conserving genetic diversity as an insurance against future need has lately become a telling argument in support of wildlife conservation, but it applies with greatest force in those countries where a much larger proportion of crop species of plant and animal has been developed from the native flora and fauna than is the case in Britain. Some wildlife species are regarded by other interests as pests, but pest control is the province of agriculture, fisheries and forestry departments. Moreover, the responsibility of the NC to advise on the 'control of the natural flora

and fauna' was lost in the NCC Act 1973. Soil conservation is connected primarily with farming and forestry, and the economic aspects of water quality are the responsibility of the Water Authorities. Use of minerals in industry and urban development has been controlled by other departments, and NCC has only an indirect interest in energy conservation.

12.1.3 The revision of statutory functions in the NCC Act 1973 does not specify their breadth of scope and purpose. The parliamentary debates on the subject published in Hansard nevertheless convey the Government's resistance to any wider interpretation of role than that already established by the former NC. In any case, the finance needed to tackle adequately the larger field of integrated resource conservation is vastly larger than that ever available to the nature conservation movement. To have sought such involvement with available funds would have been mere dabbling in the problems, whilst diluting efforts on the established fronts.

12.1.4 Nature conservation in NCC has thus inevitably been compressed into a narrower responsibility for the protection and management of wild flora, fauna and physical features for a range of purposes which can broadly be termed cultural rather than economic (see 14.2.2). Cultural purpose has always been the remit of most NGOs concerned with nature conservation: the educational function is the basis of their charitable status. Bodies such as Friends of the Earth and Greenpeace nevertheless identify with the wider role.

12.1.5 The inability to develop a broader kind of nature conservation should be regarded as the nation's failure: the opportunity was there but it was not taken. The Conservation and Development Programme for the UK has taken up the challenge again with great vigour and well deserves to succeed, but the resistances are still considerable.

12.2 Losses of the heritage of nature

12.2.1 Many critics would see the most serious failure of the conservation movement as the sheer scale of loss or damage to wildlife, its habitat and physical features that has taken place since 1949.

Although there have been some gains, in the creation of reservoirs, flooded gravel, sand and clay workings, disused stone quarries and new coniferous forests as incidental wildlife habitats and by amenity tree-planting programmes and small-scale habitat recreation, these are far outweighed by the losses. All main types of ecosystem have suffered appreciable loss, but, for some, the scale and rate have been catastrophic. The following are the estimates of the most important losses:—

12.2.1.1 Lowland neutral grasslands (including herb-rich hay meadows): 95% now lacking significant wildlife interest and only 3% left undamaged by agricultural intensification (Annex 1:5).

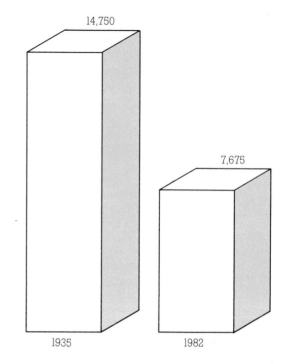

Figure 5a: Loss of permanent pasture in North Kent marshes (hectares)

14,750

7,675

1935   1982

Herb-rich hay meadow

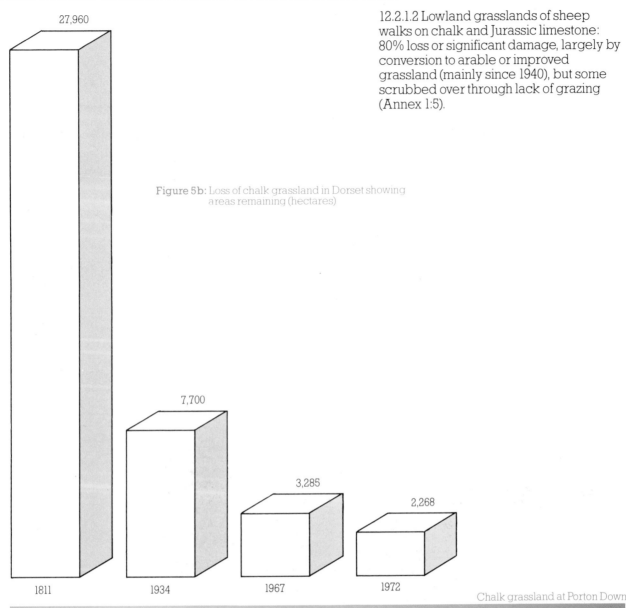

27,960

7,700

3,285

2,268

1811   1934   1967   1972

Figure 5b: Loss of chalk grassland in Dorset showing areas remaining (hectares)

12.2.1.2 Lowland grasslands of sheep walks on chalk and Jurassic limestone: 80% loss or significant damage, largely by conversion to arable or improved grassland (mainly since 1940), but some scrubbed over through lack of grazing (Annex 1:5).

Chalk grassland at Porton Down

12.2.1.3 Lowland heaths on acidic soils:
40% loss, largely by conversion to arable
or improved grassland, afforestation and
building; some scrubbed over through
lack of grazing.

Figure 5c: Losses of lowland heath

District	Date	Areas of heath (hectares)	% loss between first and last date
1. Breckland, Suffolk/Norfolk	1824	16,469	
	1950	9,268	
	1963	5,973	
	1980	4,529	73
2. Sandlings, Suffolk	1783	16,403	
	1960	1,823	
	1983	1,580	90
3. Surrey	1804	55,400	
	1983	5,901	89
4. Hampshire	1819	37,000	
	1982	18,000	51
5. Dorset	1750	39,960	
	1814	30,352	
	1896	22,663	
	1934	18,211	
	1960	10,117	
	1973	6,070	
	1978	5,832	
	1983	5,670	86
6. Lizard, Cornwall	1813	2,270	38 gain owing
	1880	3,610	to economic
	1908	3,660	depression
	1963	3,280	
	1980	2,580	31
All six districts	1830	143,250	
	1880	112,750	
	1930	82,000	
	1950	64,500	
	1980	39,450	78

Overall loss between 1950 and 1984 is 40%.

Acidic lowland heath, Dorset

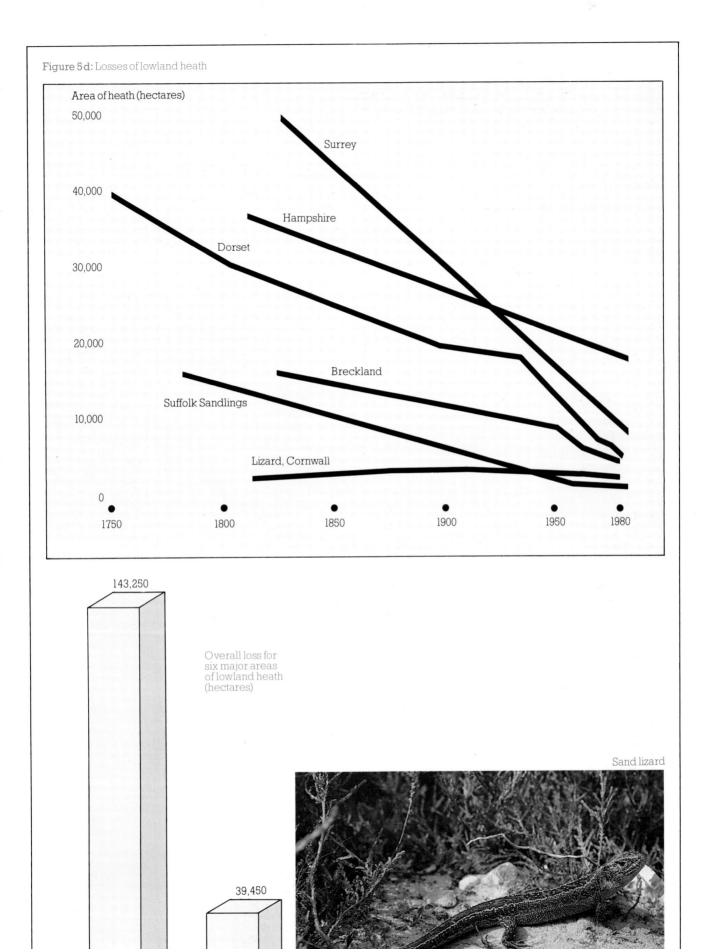

Figure 5d: Losses of lowland heath

Area of heath (hectares)

- 50,000
- 40,000
- 30,000
- 20,000
- 10,000
- 0

Surrey

Hampshire

Dorset

Breckland

Suffolk Sandlings

Lizard, Cornwall

1750 1800 1850 1900 1950 1980

143,250

Overall loss for six major areas of lowland heath (hectares)

39,450

1830 1980

Sand lizard

12.2.1.4 Limestone pavements in northern England: 45% damaged or destroyed, largely by removal of weathered surfaces for sale as rockery stone, and only 3% left undamaged (Annex 1:6).

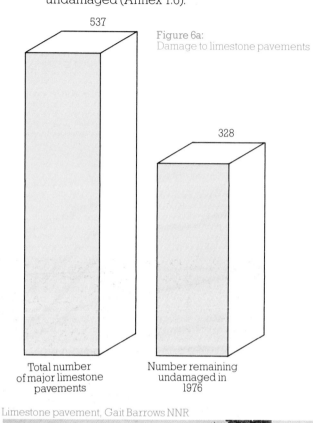

537

Figure 6a:
Damage to limestone pavements

328

Total number of major limestone pavements

Number remaining undamaged in 1976

Hart's-tongue fern

Limestone pavement, Gait Barrows NNR

12.2.1.5 Ancient lowland woods composed of native, broad-leaved trees: 30-50% loss, by conversion to conifer plantation or grubbing out to provide more farmland (Annex 1:6).

Figure 6b:
Loss of ancient semi-natural woodland in south and south-east Scotland

Region	Period	Loss %
Borders	1946-71	21
Lothian	1946-75	25
Fife	1946-75	36
Central	1946-71	25
Tayside	1946-77	30
Strathclyde (part)	1945-79	19
Dumfries & Galloway	1946-73	31

Hedges

Field boundary hedges have been removed on a large scale as part of agricultural modernisation. The scale of loss has varied widely geographically, being greatest in the cereal areas of eastern England and least in the stock-rearing districts. By using air photographs, it has been estimated that, of around 500,000 miles of hedge existing in England and Wales in 1946-47, some 140,000 miles had been removed by 1974; and all but 20,000 miles of this loss was attributable to farming.

White admiral

Lady Park Wood, Wye valley

Wood anemones and celandines

Figure 6c: Loss of ancient semi-natural woodland in some counties of England and Wales

County	Surviving area of ancient semi-natural woodland in 1983	Converted to plantation during last 50 years*	Totally destroyed during last 50 years	% converted to plantation or destroyed in the last 50 years
Avon	2810	1040	141	30
Bedfordshire	1648	943	178	40
Buckinghamshire	6809	2642	299	30
Cambridgeshire	2035	763	222	33
Cornwall	3246	2928	119	48
Essex	7252	1372	931	24
Hertfordshire	3431	2111	462	43
Humberside	767	308	110	35
Leicestershire	1614	1067	341	47
Lincolnshire	2868	3351	261	56
N. Cumbria	2524	1559	269	42
Norfolk	1410	1395	144	52
Northamptonshire	2634	3931	694	64
Northumberland	3588	3194	323	50
Oxfordshire	5656	2884	270	36
Shropshire	4133	6382	641	63
Somerset	5687	4489	426	46
Suffolk	3022	1347	483	38
Surrey	4712	2428	840	41
Clwyd	3032	2402	379	48
Gwent	3249	5568	925	67
Gwynedd	3415	3174	376	51
Pembrokeshire	1244	1286	44	52

└──────── All figures in hectares ────────┘

*In a small number of instances the base maps for the earlier period were up to 80 years old.

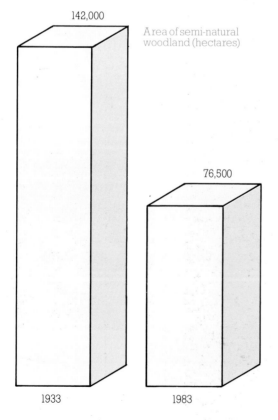

142,000

Area of semi-natural woodland (hectares)

76,500

1933   1983

Loss of ancient semi-natural woodland in 23 counties of England and Wales (hectares)

The bulk of the woodland converted to plantation has been planted with conifers, with consequent reduction or loss of wildlife interest. Woodland totally destroyed has mostly been grubbed out to create more farmland. Ancient woods are those on sites wooded since at least 1600 and often dating back to the original wildwood; semi-natural woods are those with tree and shrub layers of species native to the site.

12.2.1.6 Lowland fens, valley and basin mires: 50% loss or significant damage through drainage operations, reclamation for agriculture and chemical enrichment of drainage water (Annex 1:6).

Bogbean

Calthorpe Broad, Norfolk

3,380

Figure 6d:
Loss of East Anglian Fenland (square kilometres)

100

10

1637   1934   1984

12.2.1.7 Lowland raised mires: 60% loss or significant damage through afforestation, peat-winning, reclamation for agriculture or repeated burning (Annex 1:6).

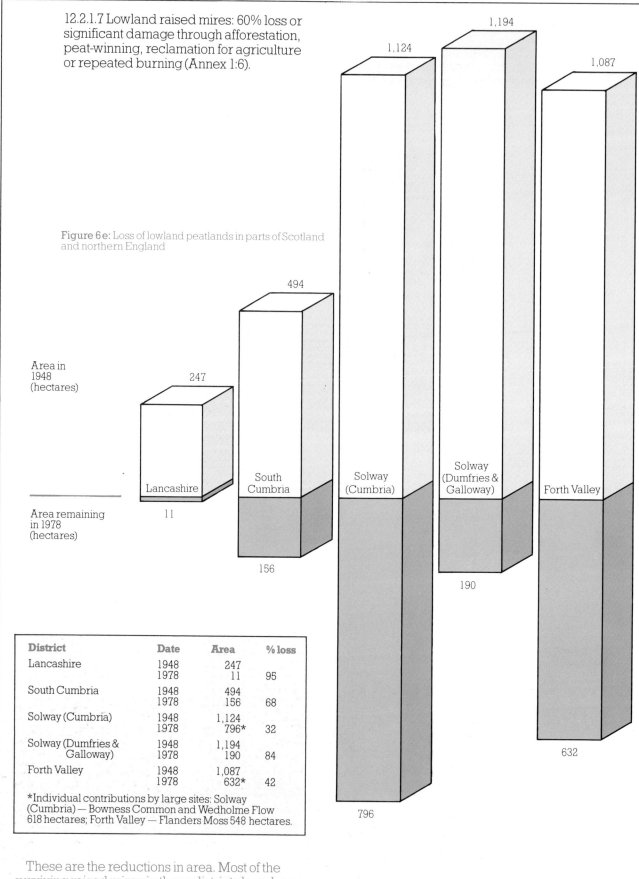

Figure 6e: Loss of lowland peatlands in parts of Scotland and northern England

Area in 1948 (hectares)

Area remaining in 1978 (hectares)

District	Date	Area	% loss
Lancashire	1948	247	
	1978	11	95
South Cumbria	1948	494	
	1978	156	68
Solway (Cumbria)	1948	1,124	
	1978	796*	32
Solway (Dumfries & Galloway)	1948	1,194	
	1978	190	84
Forth Valley	1948	1,087	
	1978	632*	42

*Individual contributions by large sites: Solway (Cumbria) — Bowness Common and Wedholme Flow 618 hectares; Forth Valley — Flanders Moss 548 hectares.

These are the reductions in area. Most of the surviving raised mires in these districts have been damaged by fire and at least marginal peat cutting. The largest complex, Thorne and Halfield Moors near Doncaster (2,630 hectares), has been almost entirely cut over for peat removal. Only a few examples, covering about 1,150 hectares in Galloway and the Highlands, have survived more or less intact.

12.2.1.8 Upland grasslands, heaths and blanket bogs: 30% loss or significant damage through coniferous afforestation, hill land improvement and reclamation, burning and over-grazing (Annex 1:7).

Figure 7a:
Loss of upland grasslands, heath and blanket bog through land-use changes between 1950 and 1980 (hectares)

4,614

3,822

1,143

5,480

Dartmoor

Brecon Beacons

Northern Snowdonia

North York Moors

Heather moorland in north-east Scotland

12.2.2 Other habitat loss and damage includes intertidal flats and saltings (agricultural and industrial reclamation), sand-dunes (afforestation, recreational pressure, agricultural reclamation), shingle beaches (construction, pebble removal), lakes and rivers (pollution, water abstraction, land drainage, acidification — Annex 1:7) and certain higher mountains (recreational pressure, especially ski developments).

Sea aster

Figure 7b: Deterioration of certain open water key sites (lakes and rivers)

Type of site	Number	Loss of value	Reason
Lakes	73	9	Nutrient enrichment (8) Acidification in peat (1)
Rivers	18	1	Dredging and pollution from fish farm
Canals	1	1	Converted to marina
Cave water bodies	4	—	
Grazing marsh ditches	3	1*	Deepened; adjoining marsh converted to arable
Total 99		12	(12%)

*Part of system still undamaged.

The above table refers only to key sites identified in 1967 and 1968 and listed in A Nature Conservation Review 1977.

Estuarine reclamation in the Wash

Saltmarsh and sand dunes on the north Norfolk coast

12.2.3 The actual flora and fauna have suffered losses in parallel. Overall, the plants and animals of habitats affected by agricultural intensification have suffered the greatest decline, that is especially those of the lowland grasslands, heaths and wetlands. Of the various groups monitored so far, the butterflies and dragonflies have shown the biggest losses. One butterfly (the large blue) became extinct in 1979, but ten more species are, out of a total British list of 55 resident breeding species (Figure 8), vulnerable or even seriously endangered, and another 13 have declined and contracted in range substantially since 1960. And of our 43 species of dragonflies, three or possibly four became extinct since 1953, six are vulnerable or endangered, and five have decreased substantially (Figure 9). These insects belong especially to habitats strongly affected by modern trends in land-use, but they also appear to be intrinsically sensitive to change. Insect biology is such that these creatures are on the whole less buffered against adversity than the vertebrates and higher plants. The possibility that butterflies and dragonflies may be indicators for wider

Swallowtail butterfly

Figure 8: Decline in resident butterfly populations in Britain since 1950

Species		Comments and reasons for decline
Adonis blue	vulnerable	Loss of chalk-grassland to ploughing; lack of grazing on many remaining sites.
Brown hairstreak	declining	Loss of hedgerows, extensive mechanical cutting, alteration of woodland edge by ploughing meadows, coniferisation, etc.
Chalkhill blue	declining	Loss of chalk grassland to ploughing and lack of grazing.
Chequered skipper	declining	Lack of woodland management caused rides to become unsuitable; reasons for loss not entirely understood.
Dark green fritillary	declining	Loss of wide woodland rides through lack of management or changes following coniferisation; loss of downland and other habitat.
Dingy skipper	declining	Loss of grasslands, lack of suitable management.
Duke of Burgundy	vulnerable	Loss of most woodland sites to coniferisation; cessation of coppicing etc; ploughing or scrubbing over of grasslands.
Grayling	declining	Loss of inland colonies; ploughing or lack of grazing of chalk grasslands; destruction or coniferisation of heaths.
Grizzled skipper	declining	Loss of grasslands and lack of suitable management.
Heath fritillary	vulnerable	Cessation of coppicing and conversion to conifers.
High brown fritillary	vulnerable	Loss of woodland glades through lack of management or coniferisation; Ploughing or 'improvement' of woodland edge meadows.
Large blue	extinct	Ploughing of grasslands, absence of grazing and cessation of gorse burning
Large tortoiseshell	endangered	Reasons for decline not understood; loss of hedgerow trees, including elm and change in agricultural landscape.
Marbled white	declining	Loss of grasslands and scrubbing over.
Marsh fritillary	vulnerable	Loss of wet meadows to modern agriculture; woodland sites lost as rides close in.
Pearl-bordered fritillary	declining	Coniferisation and cessation of coppicing.
Purple emperor	declining	Loss and fragmentation of large woods, conversion to conifers and changes in ride management.
Silver-spotted skipper	vulnerable	Loss of chalk grassland and lack of suitable grazing.
Silver-studded blue	vulnerable	Loss of open heathland and lack of suitable grazing on chalk grassland sites.
Silver-washed fritillary	declining	Abandonment of traditional forest management and effects of modern conifer forestry.
Small blue	delining	Most colonies are very small and lost to ploughing, grazing and development.
Small pearl-bordered	declining	Cessation of coppicing and conversion to conifers.
White-letter hairstreak	vulnerable	Loss of elms.
Wood white	vulnerable	Has done fairly well lately, mainly through introductions and while sites are temporarily suitable; poised for a major decline following coniferisation.

problems among the less studied groups of invertebrates is worrying. Some of the 26 species of bumblebee have certainly been seriously affected. And the implications of atmospheric pollution (i.e. acid deposition) effects for lichens and for aquatic life in more acid waters are also disturbing.

Figure 9: Decline in resident dragonfly populations in Britain since 1950

Species		Comments and reasons for decline
Coenagrion armatum	extinct	Deterioration of the Norfolk Broads.
Coenagrion scitulum	extinct	Marine flooding of East Anglian coast in 1953.
Lestes dryas	extinct	Agricultural drainage, intensive ditching, loss of ponds. (Migrants appeared in 1983 but may not succeed in permanently re-establishing.)
Oxygastra curtisii	extinct	River pollution; sensitive even to 'safe' water from sewage treatment plant.
Aeshna isosceles	endangered	Pollution of the Broads; over-management of ditches on grazing marsh including drainage improvement schemes for agriculture.
Brachytron pratense	declining	Agricultural improvement of grazing levels.
Coenagrion mercuriale	vulnerable	Very vulnerable to drainage of small flushes and streams.
Coenagrion pulchellum	declining	Agricultural improvement of grazing levels and intensive ditching.
Gomphus vulgatissimus	vulnerable	River improvement and dredging (lost from one site recently).
Leucorrhinia dubia	vulnerable	Drainage, afforestation and invasion of conifers on to adjacent heath.
Libellula fulva	vulnerable	Pollution, over-management of rivers and the Broads.
Platycnemis pennipes	declining	River improvement and water pollution.
Somatochlora arctica	vulnerable	Flush habitat affected by drainage and afforestation.
Somatochlora metallica	declining	Improvement and power craft use of canals; improvement of ponds for fishing.
Sympetrum sanguineum	declining	Loss of ponds; removal of emergent vegetation to improve fishing and amenity.

Tree lungwort

Four-spotted libellula

12.2.4 Birds are on the whole fairly resilient, and the populations of many species are prone to normal fluctuations as a result of natural processes, including the effects of weather. Yet they too are showing parallel trends in respect of the most modified habitats. At least 36 breeding species have shown appreciable long-term decline during the last 35 years as a result of habitat loss or deterioration, 30 in the lowlands and six in the uplands. New upland afforestation, especially in its early stages of growth, encourages many animals, especially birds such as the vole-feeding predators, blackgame and small passerines needing dense ground cover. The mature forest becomes important song-bird habitat, compensating to some extent for the losses of common species resulting from hedge and woodland removal in the lowlands. These gains have, however, to be set against losses of the open moorland birds, which include notable predators and waders. It is thus always necessary to evaluate the changes in terms of a balance sheet. Figure 4 gives further details on species losses.

12.2.5 Amongst the mammals, the otter has become rare or has disappeared in many parts of England and Wales, and its decline escaped notice by many naturalists. Bats in general have decreased and several of our 15 species, notably the greater horseshoe and mouse-eared bats are at risk of extinction. Others such as Bechstein's, Leisler's and the barbastelle are rare, and even the pipistrelle is no longer common. Problems are food supply, destruction of breeding and hibernation roosts and pollution. Their threatened status is reflected in the legal protection now accorded to all species. Four of our 12 reptiles and amphibians are similarly endangered. There have been local increases and extensions of range in some vertebrate populations (e.g. wild cat, and pine marten), but the overall balance of change is again on the debit side.

Top: Common long-eared bat
Bottom: Pine marten

Top: Common snipe
Bottom: Stone curlew

12.2.6 Botanical losses have been quite substantial, and include ten extinctions of species since 1930. Out of 1,423 native flowering plants and ferns, 149 (10·5%) have declined by at least 20% in 10 × 10 km grid square occurrences since 1930. Of the 149, 69 belong to wetland habitats, 32 to permanent grassland, 18 to woodland and 14 to sandy or heathland habitats. At present, 317 vascular plant species are regarded as nationally rare, occurring in only 15 or fewer 10 × 10 km grid squares. Of these, 117 (37%) have shown at least 33% decline since 1930; 34 belong to grasslands, 21 to wetlands, 19 to sandy or heathland habitats, and 14 to dry banks or shingle. Figure 10 gives further details and shows examples of decline.

Snake's-head fritillary

Early spider-orchid

Figure 10: Decline in flowering plants and ferns in Britain since 1930

Species extinctions since 1930	Approx. date of last record	Habitat and reason for extinction
Holosteum umbellatum	1930	Old walls, thatched roofs and banks; habitat destroyed.
Hydrilla verticillata	1934	Freshwater lakes, possibly water pollution.
Halimione pedunculata	1935	Salt marshes; partly reclamation.
Campanula persicifolia	1949	Open woods and commons; reason not known.
Filago gallica	1955	Dry, grassy places; habitat destruction.
Saxifraga rosacea	1960	Mountain cliffs; collecting.
Spiranthes aestivalis	1960	Southern valley bogs; draining and collecting.
Ajuga genevensis	1967	Chalk pasture and dunes; reclamation and disturbance.
Otanthus maritimus	1936	Fixed dunes and fine shingle; possibly climatic change.
Arnoseris minima	1970	Sandy arable fields; agricultural change.
Bupleurum rotundifolium	1970	Cornfields and verges; cleaning of grain seed and herbicides.
Bromus interruptus	1972	Arable fields; clearing of crop heads and herbicides.

*Introduced species

Species showing at least 20% decline since 1930

Habitat category	Number of species	Percentage of British native flora*
Dry banks, shingle	3	0·3
Arable	6	0·4
Woodlands	18	1·3
Grassland	32	2·2
Sandy areas/heaths	14	1·0
Upland	7	0.5
Wetland	69	4·8
TOTAL	149	10·5

*Totalling 1,423 species, excluding micro-species and introductions.

Nationally rare species showing at least 33% decline since 1930

Habitat category	Number of species	Percentage of total *
Dry banks, shingle	14	4·4
Arable	12	3·8
Woodlands	8	2·5
Grassland	34	10·7
Sandy areas/heaths	19	6·0
Upland	9	2·8
Wetland	21	6·6
TOTAL	117	36·8

* 317 species listed in British Red Data Book I Vascular Plants, Perring, F. H. and Farrell, L.

12.2.7 Many habitats have also suffered serious loss of visual quality without necessarily decreasing in area or losing species of plant or animal. Replacement of broad-leaved woodlands by broadleaf-conifer mixtures and the gripping (draining) of moorland are good examples of practices which are highly destructive to the appearance of wild nature in semi-natural ecosystems.

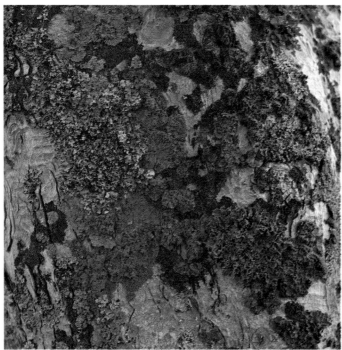

Lichens on tree trunk, Taynish NNR

Woodland on Taynish NNR

12.3 Legislation

12.3.1 On the assumption that the proposals of Cmd 7122 were essentially sound and desirable, there were some early failures in implementation. Some of the categories of areas and sites proposed for safeguard were not adopted in the 1949 legislation: the Conservation Area, Scientific Area, National Park Reserve, Geological Monument and Local Educational Reserve. This at once altered the understanding that numerous important areas should receive appropriate safeguard and required that some be added to the list of proposed NNRs or SSSIs. It also removed the possibility of giving certain fairly large areas such as Breckland a looser but adequate degree of protection from major changes in land-use. Failure to implement the recommendation for a National Park in the Norfolk Broads helped to set the scene for serious conservation problems there; but that for the South Downs came too late, since most of the open downland had been lost to war-time ploughing and enclosure.

12.3.2 Legislation has never been strong enough to give adequate support to the needs of nature conservation. The 1949 measures were based on a view which grossly under-estimated the future impacts of agriculture and forestry on the remaining area of semi-natural habitat. The 1981 provisions, although appreciably strengthened in this respect, came much too late to prevent substantial losses to our heritage of nature, and their main thrust concerns SSSIs. There is little enhancement of measures for conservation in the wider environment, which remains greatly at risk. The Act is at present backed by a resource base insufficient to deal effectively with even the administrative requirements for SSSI notification, which have produced an undesirable distortion of NCC's balance of effort. Legislation on marine nature conservation took 32 years to achieve after the creation of the NC, and setting-up of the first Marine Nature Reserve has so far been delayed by other interests.

Bure Marshes NNR

Top: Tuddenham Heath
Bottom: Wye NNR

12.4 Limitations of site safeguard

12.4.1 The nature reserve as a conservation measure has been eminently successful in saving some important areas from destruction, but certain qualifications are necessary. The maintenance or enhancement of the valued features depends on suitable management, and here it has to be admitted that some NNRs, especially those with important insect interest, have deteriorated through inadequate management. Certain estates owned by parties who in general strongly support nature conservation have been managed in ways actually inimical to this interest (e.g. conversion of broad-leaved woodland to conifers) because of economic pressures. Local Trusts often have difficulty in making sufficient management input to their reserves, usually from lack of funds, though rapid improvements are now being made through the employment of Manpower Services Commission teams.

12.4.2 The implied safeguards on some NNRs and most SSSIs are also only provisional or potential. 76 NNRs are held partly or wholly under leases, some of which expire in the near future without assurance of renewal. And while all NNRs have now also to be notified as SSSIs, the effectiveness of the 1981 Act in safeguarding SSSIs under threat of damage or loss has yet to be proved.

12.5 The Nature Conservancy and the National Parks

12.5.1 Another major failure apparent within a decade was the lack of co-ordination between the NC and the National Parks Commission in England and Wales. While the National Parks have had many benefits for nature conservation (7.9), they have achieved less than was envisaged in Cmd 7122, notably in failure to set up National Park Reserves and to

Coed Ganllwyd NNR

Rannoch Moor NNR

67

look especially to the NC for advice on conservation policy. Proposals for National Parks in Scotland were rejected, removing the possibility of co-operation. In 1968, the Countryside Commission took over the responsibility for National Parks and, with the Countryside Commission for Scotland, that for the promotion of recreation in the countryside generally. The parallel but disparate development of NCC and these two countryside agencies has continued to the present day. It is strange to many people that organisations with such closely related objectives are so distanced from each other when their interests would seem to have benefited by closer alignment. There is consultation and liaison over many issues, but not a closely integrated joint effort. One particular benefit would have been in presenting combined strength to oppose developments highly damaging to the interests of both nature conservation and scenic beauty. It is, however, true that the nature conservation and scenic amenity views of needs do not invariably coincide.

12.6 Research

12.6.1 While the research achievements of NC/NCC represent a very considerable accomplishment in terms of both basic and applied science, the overall history of research is not a happy one from the conservation viewpoint. There was an early neglect of the kinds of biological survey recommended in Cmd 7122 to record the resources of vegetation, flora and fauna and the physical features of Britain, in favour of more intellectually challenging and novel avenues of ecological research. This set a pattern which led eventually to a belief that too

Experimental Plots Monks Wood

large a part of the research programme had little if any relevance to practical conservation. Survey knowledge of wildlife resources is still patchy and inadequate overall, despite increased effort in recent years, and this shortcoming limits the urgent SSSI renotification programme. There has also been a considerable shortfall in the amount of management-orientated research, though this is partly the result of inadequate funding.

12.6.2 The splitting of the former NC in 1973 had highly damaging effects on the scientific competence of its successor, NCC. There is probably now a more effective return on research per unit cost, a better overall orientation to conservation needs and a greater flexibility for dealing with new projects than before; but these advantages have to be set against the serious decline in the absolute amount of research, the loss of the enormous reservoir of scientific knowledge and experience once available for both internal and external advice, and severance of the invaluable proximity between those facing practical problems and those who could provide the answers. Moreover since 1973 NCC's residual funding of research has been almost halved in real terms. Shortage of capacity limits completion of survey, the adequate development of habitat monitoring, most areas of ecological research, socio-economic studies and scientific data-handling facilities. While NERC is still doing a considerable amount of back-up work on its own funds, the planned support of research to nature conservation has declined considerably. Technical advice within NCC now has to be provided by a score of scientists in place of the 200 once available in the former NC. The joint Habitat Teams of regional and research staff were lost, and NERC funding of research studentships since 1973 has given low priority to nature conservation topics.

12.6.3 Slowness in establishing a computerised conservation data base, especially in relation to important sites, must be accounted a failure within the conservation movement as a whole, but of NC/NCC in particular.

12.7 Shortage of resources

12.7.1 Although the growth of the nature conservation movement has been instanced as a success (11.6), many people also see failure in the limited growth of certain parts. Many local Nature Conservation Trusts have little money and so have a more limited capacity for practical work than if they were able to employ the staff necessary to mobilise the volunteer potential more effectively. By far the greatest disappointment, however, is that successive governments have continued to support their official conservation agency with a mere pittance from the national budget. Britain at present allocates 0·01% of public expenditure (0·005% of the Gross Domestic Product), or the price of a cup of tea a year for each of its inhabitants, to sustain NCC. The task which the nature conservation movement now has to tackle has been enormously increased since 1945 **more by the policies of successive governments than by any other factor.** Despite relatively hard times at present, Britain is still an exceedingly wealthy country, and it has received a quite unprecedented windfall in the form of North Sea oil. Yet its financial provision for the care of one of its most priceless assets can only be described as miserly and short-sighted. Figure 11 conveys the sense of government priority for nature conservation.

Figure 11: Gross domestic product and employment in the United Kingdom in 1981

Industry	£ million	%	People employed thousands	%
Agriculture, forestry and fishing	4,867	2·3	657	2·7
Petroleum and natural gas	11,972	5·7	345	
Other mining and quarrying	3,455	1·6		1·4
Manufacturing	49,916	23·7	6,929	28·3
Construction	13,545	6·4	1,672	6·9
Gas, electricity and water	6,670	3·2	347	1·4
Total output industries	90,425	42·9	9,950	40·7
Total service industries (including tourism)	118,525 (6,925)	63·8 (3·3)	14,418 (c.1,500)	59·2 6·2
Adjustments	14,150	6·6	—	—
Gross domestic product at factor cost	210,788	100·0		
Total employed civil population			24,368	

Data from **Britain 1983: an official handbook.** HMSO.

Total public expenditure by programme £ million cash

	1983-1984 estimated out-turn	1984-1985 plans	1985-1986 plans
Social security	35,324	37,207	39,520
Defence	15,716	17,031	18,060
Health and personal social services	14,688	15,421	16,250
Education and science	13,356	13,052	13,450
Scotland (Countryside Commission for Scotland)	6,767 (3)	6,863 (3)	6,980
Trade, industry, energy and employment	6,080	5,609	4,700
Law order and protective services	4,681	4,901	5,130
Transport	4,560	4,372	4,690
Northern Ireland	3,799	4,032	4,220
Other environmental services (mainly DoE) (including Nature Conservancy Council, Countryside Commission, National Park Grant)	3,787 (13) (13) (7)	3,451 (14) (13) (7)	3,540
Housing	2,760	2,496	2,610
Wales	2,587	2,585	2,680
Government lending to nationalised industries	2,500	1,881	1,140
Overseas aid and other overseas services	2,294	2,283	2,520
Agriculture, fisheries, food and industry	2,087	2,048	1,920
Other public services	1,666	1,788	1,870
Common services	950	1,105	1,180
Arts and libraries	624	599	620
Local authority current expenditure not allocated to programmes (England)		660	400
Special sales of assets	−1,200	−1,900	−2,000
Reserve	100	2,750	3,750
General allowance for shortfall	−300		
Planning total	122,826	128,234	133,230

Figures for local authority expenditure on nature conservation are not separately identifiable.

Data from the government's expenditure plans 1984-1985 to 1986-1987. HM Treasury, February 1984.

12.7.2 With very few exceptions, for example the National Trust and RSPB, the voluntary movement has not yet mobilised financial resources to the extent that might have been expected, given the million or so people keenly interested in nature conservation. It is surprising that examples from the USA have not given greater stimulus in this respect.

13

Conclusions

13.1 Both the achievements and the shortcomings of past nature conservation performance have been considerable, depending on the vantage point of appraisal. The main value of an analysis of achievements is, however, **to use it as insight for the future,** by recognising what worked, what failed and why, where the problems now lie and how they should be tackled henceforth, with better results than in the past.

13.2 The development of nature conservation in Britain described in Part I and analysed in Part II indicates a record of success. There is now a large and supportive body of concerned opinion, a countrywide framework of nature reserves covering 1% of Britain, and a mechanism for protecting at least another 6% of the countryside. Important scientific successes have also been gained and a professionalism achieved in the subject. Yet, despite all this, there is a strong sense that the nature conservation movement has failed to achieve enough, notably in allowing the scale of post-war attrition of nature depicted in 12.2. The losses of habitats, communities, species and physical features since 1949 are such that, while the methods of site safeguard are generally capable of success, **the overall programme for their application to the protection of important areas has been hopelessly inadequate.** It has been too little and too late. The wider countryside programme has, in its total effect, been still less effectual in dealing with the central problem of loss. And, while Britain still has a high standing overseas in the technology of nature conservation, its international reputation as a practitioner has slipped significantly in recent years.

13.3 Some of the particular failures identified in Section 12 are attributable partly to circumstance and partly to unfavourable government decisions. It is, however, arguable that government policy largely mirrors public demand, and that the demand for nature conservation was not perceived as sufficiently large and urgent. The blame is then upon the conservationists themselves for not having demonstrated their cause with better effect. They have not persuaded the nation that nature merits more than a very lowly place in its affairs, in terms of financial support (Figure 11). Past performance also reveals a reluctance to learn how to cope with the politics of competition in the use of natural resources. On the one hand, the conservationists were not energetic enough in 'selling their product' as a major concern of society and showed a tendency to timidity in dealing with more powerful interests. And on the other, they either under-estimated the portents for the great increase in human impact on nature, or they were slow to gather the growing evidence and draw attention to it in the most effective way. Some perceptive individuals and groups saw all this clearly enough and made the right response, but the nature conservation movement as a whole lagged behind and showed a disastrous lack of cohesion in its total effort.

13.4 The lessons are clear. We are compelled to regard the trends identified in 12.2 as alarming and to use the measures available for reducing or halting them with all possible vigour. No one could deny that the acceptance of compromise is essential to the functioning of a democratic society. But in nature conservation the great compromise has been made already, through the surrender of so much of our heritage of nature to development for the national good. Since 1949, when nature conservation first existed in organised form, it has been compromising all the time, often indeed with little choice, by paying regard to the needs of other land-use interests. The advantage has been predominantly in favour of the development interests. In some parts of Britain there is little if anything left to compromise about, and we feel that the time has come for other interests to pay regard to the needs of nature conservation.

13.5 The strategy for nature conservation will, accordingly, pay close attention not only to the devices and procedures for achieving its objectives, but also to the manner in which they are used. It will seek a new co-ordination and unity between the component bodies of the movement and aim to project a more powerful appeal to the nation. Financial support for conservation will grow in close relation to society's increase in concern for nature. Communication in its various aspects is all-important to success. And in conveying the conservation message, we should exploit

the truth that nature is its own most
eloquent spokesman when given the
opportunity.

Part III
The future direction of nature conservation

Reconsideration of rationale

14.1 In looking forward, the first task is to enquire whether any part of the framework defining previous practice has changed significantly. This framework consists of the accepted purposes of nature conservation, the remit of the various practitioners, the range of problems involved and, hence, the sequence of objectives to guide action.

14.2 Purpose and remit

14.2.1 The broad, integrated concept of natural resource conservation so ably expounded in Cmd 7122 has been further developed and refined in the World Conservation Strategy (WCS). This definitive statement stresses the need to maintain essential ecological processes and life support systems, to preserve genetic diversity, and to ensure the sustainable utilisation of species and ecosystems. Emphasis is thus on the global socio-economic relevance of renewable resource conservation, though the WCS specifically avoids the problems of human population growth. It promotes the philosophy that, with careful planning and control, conservation and development can be compatible activities. A group of interested parties has produced the Conservation and Development Programme for the UK as a response to the WCS, but extending concern from use of resources to urban and industrial renewal, education and ethics. This programme is a national package for socio-economic improvement through integrated natural resource use. It is, however, unofficial, and government has yet to show what support it is prepared to give.

14.2.2 To some people, the broad concept of integrated resource management is the true interpretation of nature conservation purpose. An approach of this scope has, however, not been possible for the nature conservation movement in Britain, for the reasons discussed in 12.1. Since these same reasons still apply, it seems best to accept that the proper role for NCC and most of the NGOs is to practise nature conservation according to a definition of purpose which is primarily **cultural,** that is **the conservation of wild flora and fauna, geological and physiographic features of Britain for their scientific, educational, recreational, aesthetic and inspirational value.** The term cultural should not be misconstrued: it is used here in the broadest sense as referring to the whole mental life of a nation. This cultural purpose shades imperceptibly into that which is clearly economic, that is, dealing with aspects of resource utilisation providing the commodities for material existence and regulated by commercial factors. It is, perhaps, undesirable to distinguish sharply between the two, for both are necessary to quality of life, and many nature conservation activities serve both purposes (see Figure 12). The conservation of genetic variability in wildlife also spans the two aspects. There must, nevertheless, be clear understanding that the range of purpose central to this document is weighted heavily to the cultural end of the spectrum, because this is the balance of concern within NCC and the NGOs. Conversely, commercial interests have a concern for the conservation of nature which is heavily weighted towards economic purpose. The cultural interest in nature has itself a considerable economic value in total, but this is mainly incidental and not a direct intention.

14.2.3 Science has an important place within this range of cultural purpose, as an end in itself and also as a means of supporting the technical practice of nature conservation. The advancement of science will continue to be one of the main reasons for conserving wildlife and physical features, as the medium within which natural scientists can pursue their quest for knowledge. Geological and physiographic conservation are mainly orientated towards scientific purpose including the training of earth scientists. And science clearly has a certain importance in serving the economic purpose of conservation. Yet by far the greatest weight, in terms of numbers of interested people, lies at the other end of the spectrum of public interest and is expressed in simple enjoyment and inspiration from contact with nature. While this interest merges into the still more diffuse values of landscape and scenic beauty in the countryside, the dividing line is that nature conservation must deal specifically with the tangible phenomena of flora, fauna and physical features and the ways in which these are important to people. And the rationale of cultural purpose has to accept also that many people regard even this concern for the non-material value of nature to man as a utilitarian view, which they reject in favour of a belief that man himself has a duty to respect nature in its own right.

14.2.4 This view of cultural purpose identifies the nature conservation bodies as a sectional or partisan interest and sets them aside from any neutral or adjudicatory role in the use of natural resources. They nevertheless subscribe whole-heartedly to the concept of integrated resource use, both as a rational and ethical principle for a civilised society and as a means of having their own sectional interest taken more fully into account in a fair and balanced way. They believe that the planned integration of conservation with development to serve a range of needs is better than the present adversarial system of competing interests; and they accordingly wish to promote the broader view of conservation by giving their support and advocacy to the Conservation and Development Programme for the UK. This is different from a wish for direct executive responsibility in the adjudicatory role which integrated conservation would require in practice. As well as supporting attempts to harmonise conflicting interests, the nature conservation bodies will draw attention to wider conservation problems evidently neglected by other parties whose concern they should be. They will also engage in issues of important indirect relevance to nature conservation and in those where the concern for nature is only one part of a much wider environmental interest.

14.2.5 By the same token, the nature conservation bodies will maintain a close interest in the economics of land and resource use in general, so that they are aware of the forces which influence various kinds of development affecting nature. They have to scrutinise the validity of economic arguments used to justify inimical environmental impacts and to be able to weigh such factors against the benefits of conservation purposes, when advancing their own cause.

14.3 Conservation problems today: relevance of the change in the socio-economic scene

14.3.1 The nature conservation movement made its greatest single advance during the period of post-war planning and reconstruction which so powerfully expressed the wish of people for a better future. It grew with the post-war rise in economic prosperity, and the increase in leisure opportunities, personal disposable income and mobility. The official nature conservation agency increased steadily in size, though it was always constrained by stringency towards what government perceived as a minority interest. The voluntary sector grew more rapidly, especially during the period of economic boom during the 1960s and the early 1970s. Public interest in nature is now at its highest level ever.

Figure 12: Relationships between different aspects of natural resource conservation

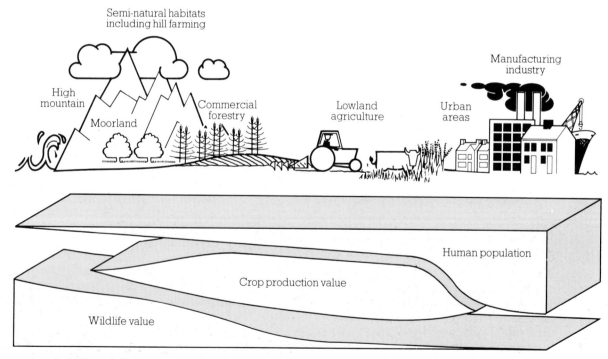

Protection of wildlife and physical features for scientific study, recreation and enjoyment, genetic and geological.

Conservation of soils, nutrients and water for production of food and timber crops.

Management of non-renewable resources, energy, water and air for industrial production and urban quality of life.

14.3.2 Growth of economic prosperity involved substantial increase in virtually all those activities which result in utilisation of environmental resources, whether for agriculture, forestry, water use, mineral exploitation, urban-industrial-transport expansion, energy generation or recreation. Defence use of land is perhaps the only major activity which has remained at a fairly steady level since 1945. The damaging impact of human activity on nature has thus increased at a time when interest in maintaining nature as a cultural resource was growing. The result has been to generate the now well-recognised conflict between development and nature conservation which stems from the sectional, non-integrated approach.

14.3.3 Although most of the major land and resource use activities have created substantial problems for nature conservation, agriculture has been overwhelmingly the most important because of the sheer geographical scale of its impact. Loss and damage to nature from farming developments have been severe during the last 35 years, largely because of government policy to maximise domestic food production, now reinforced by the Common Agricultural Policy of the EEC which created a guaranteed, open-ended market for certain food stuffs. The public subsidisation of agricultural improvements which cause wildlife habitat loss is the most debated conservation issue of the present time. It is now expanding into remote parts of Scotland and Wales, as EEC and national funds are provided for support to marginal hill and croftland farming. Current attempts to modify the CAP for economic reasons offer a challenge to the UK government to build environmental objectives into revised land-use policies, and thus to promote the approach of the UK Conservation and Development Programme.

14.3.4 Forestry has caused much loss and damage to important wildlife sites, especially in the lowlands through replacement of ancient broad-leaved woodland by conifer plantations. Coniferous afforestation of open moorland and heath has caused a shifting balance in wildlife composition, which is sometimes unfavourable and is increasingly creating conflict over SSSIs. Government policy reflects the continual pressure by forestry interests for expansion of the afforestation of plantable land, almost wholly with conifers; but if agriculture should happen to retract in future, there will be opportunities for further, more diverse afforestation.

Blanket afforestation in Galloway

77

14.3.5 Other interests are likely to impinge adversely as they have done in the past. Estuarine reclamation schemes and barrages, new power stations and other energy developments, water supply, road and airfield construction, spread of conurbations and industry, mining and quarrying, peat-winning, waste tipping, new forms of pollution and intrusive recreational developments are likely to remain on the standard list of conservation problems. The annual losses of farmland to other developments exacerbate the difficulties for nature conservation by causing agriculture to compensate for the deficit through further land reclamation and intensification of crop production.

14.3.6 Projections of future socio-economic trends are highly relevant to the issue of these impacts and the resulting conflicts of interests. The once optimistic prediction of increasing leisure opportunities is likely to be expressed into the foreseeable future partly as continuing if not increasing unemployment. And as Britain's oil resources approach exhaustion, pressure for the further development and exploitation of our natural resources is likely to increase. To compound the problem, the geographical distribution of personal wealth and usable leisure (i.e. spare-time mobility) is extremely uneven within Britain, for the bulk of the human population lives in the towns and cities. This means that support for nature conservation is very uneven geographically and tends to be inversely correlated with the amount of natural and semi-natural habitat. The problem is especially acute in the Scottish Highlands and Islands where a small human population with severe economic problems looks hopefully at the potential productive value of a huge area of 'undeveloped' land. Conversely there has been a great upsurge of interest in the development of nature conservation activity with the urban environment.

14.3.7 The general pressures from land-use developments thus become reinforced by rural socio-economic problems. In the Highlands and Islands, nature reserves and SSSIs have been attacked as 'sterilisation of land', with loss of potential revenue and job opportunities. EEC support for development of marginal agriculture is viewed as a valuable social subsidy to counter depopulation of remote areas, and conservationists' anxieties are regarded as unacceptable interference by people who do not have to live in these problem areas and whose contact with them is at best only seasonal. Nature conservation becomes equated with anti-development attitudes held by people who mostly belong to better-off parts of the country. Nor is this kind of issue simply a regional one. For example, all over Britain, land drainage has developed a momentum sometimes unrelated to any real economic validity it may possess. Moorland and hill draining has been shown to be an operation which cannot possibly justify its costs. Likewise, much of the pesticides and wildlife problem stemmed from the aggressive marketing activities of the chemical manufacturers and distributors.

14.3.8 There is a growing polarisation between the largely urban population seeking recreational use and aesthetic enjoyment in the countryside, as well as needing its food, and the rural landowners and occupiers whose livelihoods depend on this land and who regard themselves as the main practitioners of conservation, by right of experience, dedication and possession (see also Sections 1 and 6). As the adverse effects of agriculture and forestry on wild nature have increased and become more widely known, there has been growing public concern over the extent to which such impacts are underwritten by the taxpayer. For economic reasons, there is also interest in examining the cost-benefit validity of agricultural developments (e.g. conversion of grazing-marsh to arable and reclamation of moorland and saltmarsh) when all the elements of such support are included as a cost in the analysis. Very little development of previously unproductive land for either farming or forestry would take place nowadays without direct or indirect state subsidy. And the bulk of this subsidy is paid by the urban sector of society and derived from industrial and commercial wealth. The rural and urban sectors are thus interdependent within our socio-economic system.

14.3.9 Since its beginning, nature conservation has depended greatly on the goodwill and expertise of those who occupy and manage the land, and it will clearly continue to do so. These owners and land occupiers should, however, recognise that modern land-use methods have fundamentally altered their own relationship with nature and that this is the basic conservation problem. While they may continue to be good conservationists in maintaining their land in good heart for crop production, they are increasingly responsible for its decline in wildlife and landscape value. It is a simple but unfortunate truth that, from the nature conservation viewpoint, most modern uses of land, water and living organisms for economic purposes have adverse effects on both wildlife and the physical environment. Earlier forms of agriculture, forestry and fisheries made lighter demands on the productive capacity of the land and water and, while removing some original types of wildlife habitat, they tended incidentally to create other new and valuable types. Some plants and animals can live in habitats heavily modified or actually formed by human management of the land, and certain species now largely depend on the continuation of certain long-established practices, such as woodland coppicing and traditional hay meadow management, which are beneficial to many herbs and insects.

14.3.10 Low-input/low-output land use systems usually leave plenty of room for species other than those directly managed as the crop. On arable land, the old Norfolk Four Course rotation was beneficial to wildlife. The modern approach has been to use technology to maximise the productive capacity of the land or water, and hence the energy and nutrient flow, through the crop species. Apart from soil organisms, most other plants and animals feed on or compete with the crop species and so have to be suppressed. Others again have a food chain relationship with pest species and so disappear with them. Unneeded habitats such as hedges, ponds and ditches are removed; fields have been joined to make fewer, larger units; grassland is converted to arable, or the native herbs and grasses replaced by commercial grasses; and all kinds of uncultivated land are 'reclaimed' to provide more farmland. Fertilisers and pesticides are used in large amounts and can create their own wildlife problems. Increasingly, the farmed countryside comes to resemble a rural production line, in which the over-riding goal is efficiency measured as an output/labour ratio.

14.3.11 It would be wrong to imply that all farming is now a matter of 'prairies', monocultures and intensive livestock rearing. There is clearly a wide range of variation from the most highly developed arable and livestock farms to the marginal upland farms and Highland crofts. A journey across the heart of lowland England gives the impression that there is plenty of wildlife habitat left. Generalisations about farming also overlook individual exceptions, and the many ways in which farmers are contributing positively to nature conservation are described in Section 6. The countrywide balance of agricultural effects on nature is, nevertheless, adverse, and it is this overall trend which is causing increasing tension with wildlife interests. The goodwill of those who own and work on the land towards nature and its conservation is thus in danger of becoming a diminishing asset.

Agricultural landscape in the Chilterns

14.3.12 Industrial development has has a more localised direct impact on nature through its contribution to the built environment, and there is a good deal of industrial waste land with potential for restoration as wildlife habitat. It has long been known that the acidity in smoke from burning of fossil fuels in urban-industrial areas has a damaging effect on certain kinds of vegetation in the vicinity. Lichens are especially sensitive, and some species have declined markedly in and around the main urban and industrial districts, and some mosses have also decreased. The building of tall smoke stacks has extended the fall-out area of wet acidic deposition, and there is now widespread concern through many parts of Europe over the problem of 'acid rain'. In this country the main anxiety is that this acidification may be extending in parts of western and northern Britain with an internationally important and pollution-sensitive lichen flora and that acidity is increasing in lake and river systems in certain areas (especially those with extensive conifer plantations). Evidence of adverse effects on aquatic wildlife is growing. The problem has major socio-economic overtones; power stations are regarded as the major source of acidic deposition, but it is claimed that significant reduction in emissions would greatly increase the cost of electricity. Nuclear energy offers a smoke-free alternative, but creates its own pollution problems and anxieties.

14.3.13 While conservationists have enlarged the sympathy for their cause, there is a powerful body of resistance in some quarters, now and then expressed as open hostility by some individuals. There is increased environmental awareness in Britain over such issues as pollution and resource depletion. Industry has gradually conceded its responsibility to reduce pollution and there is more acceptance of the 'developer pays' principle, though the current problems with acid deposition and straw burning show that there is a long way to go on this score. And, while the UK Conservation and Development Programme has found a formula for the integration of conservation with development, the belief held by most industrialists, agriculturalists, politicians and economists — that economic salvation depends on growth — continues to fuel a widespread view that nature conservation is inhibitory to progress. The still worse immediate problem is, however, likely to be that of unemployment. The future direction of the nature conservation movement must recognise the relevance of these burning social issues and show sensitivity towards them. Objectives and strategy have to address a much larger and vastly better informed audience than

35 years ago, but on issues with a heightened political content.

14.4   **Main principles for the way ahead**
14.4.1 The analysis in Part II shows these approaches which have been successful, and these will have to continue to form the framework of future strategy. Yet it is possible to sharpen and strengthen their thrust in many ways, in developing a programme likely to achieve the maximum possible success for our cause. In particular, the nature conservation movement now has the immensely reassuring knowledge that it represents a major area of public interest and support and so has a duty as well as a right to take a strong and vigorous stance on the issues involved. Given the foregoing conclusions on purpose and problems, the wildlife and physical features of Britain represent an immensely valuable but highly vulnerable and much threatened cultural resource, in addition to their utility as an economic asset.

14.4.2 There is already a heavily depleted national heritage of nature. Britain has lost a great deal of its former wildlife and more fragile physical features through human activities, and forward projection of the recent rate of loss suggests that it will lose much more, unless the continuing trend can be abated by more effective measures. The seriousness of recent losses and the portents for their continuation force the nature conservation movement to contest further depletion, though recognising the impossibility of stopping it completely. The paramount need is thus to minimise further loss and to restore something of what has already been lost. In the highly developed lowlands we do not believe that any further losses to the remnants of wild nature should be allowed. In the western and northern districts and on the coast where semi-natural habitat is still extensive, the nature conservation bodies will wish to have a larger say than hitherto over developments likely to cause further losses.

14.4.3 Our strategy necessarily deals with means of reducing or preventing the damaging effects of other land and natural resource use activities. It therefore requires that nature conservation be increasingly recognised by the nation as a valid land and natural resource use activity in its own right, and well able to take its place alongside the rest within a total programme for the integrated use of Britain's natural assets. Competition or conflict with other interests will not go away of their own accord, but their overall seriousness could be substantially reduced if the priorities for nature conservation received more sympathetic recognition — for instance, by minimising adverse development on the areas of highest nature interest and maximising it on the areas of lowest interest. It also follows that more support, especially financial, will have to be forthcoming for nature conservation if there is to be any appreciable improvement on past performance. This in turn would be helped by an increasing appreciation of the values and needs of nature conservation by all sectors of the community. A primary need is for the movement to increase still further the number and effectiveness of its own supporters so that collectively they become a stronger lobby.

14.4.4 Whereas at one time opposing interests were willing to accept the nature conservation arguments, they are increasingly hiring experts with a brief to demolish them; they must accordingly expect similar treatment in regard to their own arguments. Since virtually all of the developments so inimical to nature are justified in the name of socio-economic value and need, we shall in future keep a keenly critical eye on the cogency of the actual arguments used. To this end, it will be necessary to acquire competence in the relevant fields of expertise. We shall also seek to justify the alternative value of conserving instead of exploiting natural features in competitive situations, though a longer-term aim must be to reduce the frequency of collision of interests.

14.4.5 Confrontation could be reduced by persuading government to modify some of its land-use policies, especially for agriculture and forestry, in such ways that the social objectives underlying these policies are maintained acceptably whilst taking greater account of environmental needs. The nature conservation movement should make realistic proposals for direct and indirect creation of job opportunities through its own activities, such as work on site management and the promotion of leisure-time interest in nature as an aspect of tourism and recreation. It is a matter of finding ways in which nature can serve the needs of people, including the rural community, but without recourse to damaging exploitation. The Conservation and Development Programme has analysed conflict of interest within the broader issue of total resource conservation and made constructive proposals for dealing with the problems. The nature conservation movement should carefully consider the relevance of these proposals to its own concerns, in understanding the reasons for conflict and the desirable solutions which will avoid compromising its objective of minimising further losses to nature.

14.4.6 The concern to save what is left is bound to be a major preoccupation into the future, but it should not blind other attempts to think about the enhancement of the resource of nature. The techniques of re-creation and reintroduction should be learned and applied increasingly as opportunity allows. This positive conservation, which is at present embryonic, should be used to restore both habitats and species which past human activity has destroyed. It is especially appropriate to the urban environment, where the demand is so great and the result so beneficial; but it can also be used to regain some of the lost wildlife and habitat almost anywhere. And, in so far as some developments, such as reafforestation and estuarine barrage schemes, provide changed opportunities for wildlife, these must be turned to good account. This approach also fosters co-operation with land-users in general. There should eventually come a time when the present phase of largely defensive activity is reduced as nature conservation begins to regain lost ground. This approach should not, however, become an excuse for ignoring the threat to existing nature. There should be no misunderstanding about the fact that re-created habitats are usually second-best, compared with the originals. It is seldom possible to restore ecosystems with the full richness of their former species complement, particularly in regard to the more primitive plants and invertebrates. For this reason, nature conservationists must always have a primary concern for saving the ancient remnants, however puzzling and outmoded an obsession this may appear to many laymen.

15

Future objectives and strategy for nature conservation in Britain

15.1 **The primary objective of nature conservation is to ensure that the national heritage of wild flora and fauna and geological and physiographic features remains as large and diverse as possible, so that society may use and appreciate its value to the fullest extent.** The broad framework for the nature conservation plan of campaign to meet this goal up to the year 2000 is presented as ten main themes, representing strategic objectives. The ten themes overlap and intergrade, and all are essential to the overall programme. They are, however, presented in order of projected cost, and the priorities accorded to each will depend on the people and organisations involved. Each theme is sub-divided into topics representing third-order objectives, to be developed in more detailed planning, and within which an ordering of priorities is desirable. This analysis does not attempt to detail the separate needs and methods of physical feature, wildlife habitat and species conservation: these tactical prescriptions belong to the stage of detail planning.

15.2 **Theme 1: Sites of special importance to nature conservation**

15.2.1 The strict safeguard of the most important areas under some kind of protected status is unquestionably the most powerful and cost-effective tool of nature conservation and should therefore continue to be the cornerstone of practice. Nature interest is most concentrated here (Figure 13) so that return per unit cost is high. Such protection amounts to a guarantee that management of the area for

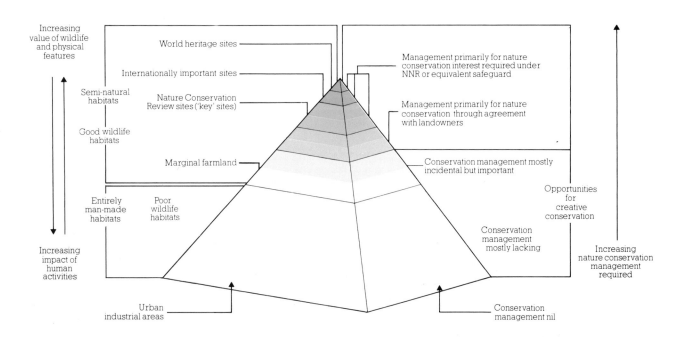

Figure 13: Nature conservation management strategy for terrestrial wildlife

The pyramid represents the total area of Great Britain. The intensity of colour shading indicates the level of nature value and the degree of conservation management needed to maintain this value.

its wildlife or physical feature interest as **the primary land-use** will be sustained indefinitely. It is best to provide such guarantee through a formal designation, notably nature reserve, preferably supported by legal status. Freehold ownership of nature reserves by conservation interests has also proved to be by far the most satisfactory of the tenure arrangements in achieving the required degree of protection. Long-term leases at low cost are the next best option.

15.2.2 Management of land or water primarily for nature conservation does not necessarily mean that use for other purposes is prevented or negated, though, in the present age of intensifying land-use, it has increasingly tended to constrain development because of the incompatibilities involved. Nature reserve management is often entirely compatible with, or in some cases actually depends on, traditional management for agriculture, forestry or game, and so it can continue to provide a certain level of economic yield. The value of nature reserves as scientific, educational and recreational assets is part of their understood purpose. The charge, sometimes heard, that nature reserves are a 'sterilisation' of land is thus totally invalid. They are, nevertheless, sometimes an obstacle to certain types of land-use development intended to produce a higher level of profit and employment.

15.2.3 The 1981 provisions for defence of SSSIs in relation to proposed damaging operations recognise that existing land-use is usually appropriate nature conservation management of these sites and that need for further protection arises when change in land-use is imminent. It is mostly measures for increasing productivity that fall into the category of damaging operations. The number of SSSIs that will need to be thus defended is uncertain and, especially since SSSI status is no guarantee of adequate protection, the nature reserve acquisition programme will have to continue in parallel. The SSSI mechanism is nevertheless valuable in giving a first line of defence to important sites, and the section 28 and 29 provisions should be rigorously applied.

15.2.4 It is important that the planned expansion of the nature reserve acquisition programme and the protection of all SSSIs should be acceptable to the nation as a legitimate primary use of land for nature conservation. Collectively, the national total of protected areas should be large and varied enough to guarantee the survival of a necessary minimum of Britain's wildlife and wild features. The

Muir of Dinnet NNR

Southern marsh-orchid

size and distribution of this target can be estimated by several criteria. First, there is the enormously wide variation in the ecosystems, flora, fauna and geological and physiographic features spread through our country; and the need to represent an adequate sample of this diversity, in terms of types and species, requires selection of a large number and wide scatter of sample locations. Some plants and animals, and their communities, have a critical minimum size for survival, and for many animals the probability of survival is also closely linked to their ability to move around from one place to another. The extent of habitat may affect its viability and that of associated species. Protected areas may also form reservoirs of wildlife which help to maintain species' populations in the wider environment. Finally, there is the actual need of interested people to be able to see important wildlife areas, not only when on holiday or through special long trips but also within easier reach of their homes. This creates a public demand factor strongly influencing requirements for protected areas.

15.2.5 The process of evaluation to select the areas worthy of protection, and especially the definition of criteria for SSSI selection, has taken account of all these factors in trying to be as objective as possible and to set consistent standards. The public demand element is, however, not constant but growing, so that the protected areas may also need to increase. Their present extent covers an overall 7% of Britain. A Geological Conservation Review, now virtually completed, has identified a considerable additional number of geological and physiographic sites worthy of SSSI status. The NCC is examining some 1,200 additional suggested new biological SSSIs and trying to identify all the remaining areas of SSSI quality. Allowing for proposals in the pipeline, for the estimated number of sites likely to be discovered on unsurveyed land, for under-studied flora and fauna (mosses, liverworts, lichens, fungi, algae and many invertebrate groups), the total area of Britain over which there should be special safeguards for nature will be about 10%. This will include regional variation from 5% to 20% according to intensity of land-use development. This seems a reasonable total, bearing in mind that existing land-use will continue over most of this land, that the bulk of the area concerned consists of unproductive coast or upland and that much of it lies within National Parks, Areas of Outstanding Natural Beauty or National Scenic Areas (see Figure 14). It should however be regarded as a **minimum** total and will require revision to a higher percentage if the losses to nature continue unacceptably.

15.2.6 The further development of the protected area programme needs careful planning, with the following main elements:—

Figure 14: Representation of major habitat types within key sites for biological nature conservation

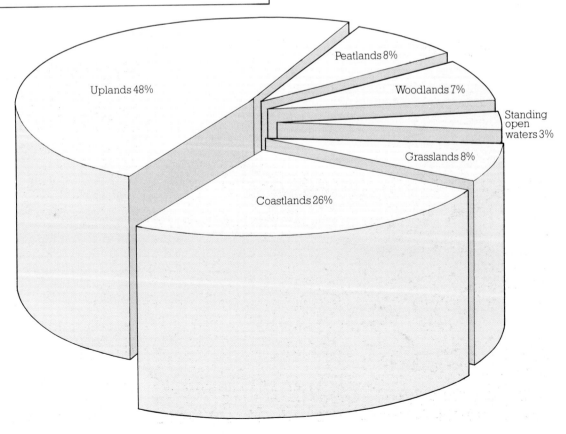

15.2.6.1 Give priority to early completion of national survey of biological and physical features, to identify remaining unscheduled areas qualifying for special protection and management. This includes completion of SSSI selection and notification by NCC and also identification of urban sites of wildlife conservation interest.

15.2.6.2 Select further areas to establish as nature reserves. These include NNRs designated by NCC (based on sites identified in **A Nature Conservation Review**) and non-statutory reserves of NGOs and others. Planned acquisition programmes should be set out, and periodic reviews incorporated.

15.2.6.3 Provide for response (especially by NCC) to sections 28 and 29 of the Wildlife and Countryside Act 1981; NCC must react to all proposals for damaging operations on SSSIs, with resultant management agreements, or site purchase. This is a reactive element in the programme, so that budgeting is problematical and progress depends on factors outside the control of the conservation bodies.

15.2.6.4 Campaign to persuade other parties (local authorities, government departments and agencies, public utilities, industrial/commercial enterprises and private individuals) to enlarge the number of protected areas already established by them, in consultation with the conservation bodies. This links with the approach under 15.3.3 and is especially relevant to establishment of reserves on urban sites below the quality of SSSI.

15.2.6.5 Set up a monitoring system to detect and measure changes in SSSIs, and the success of the 1981 Act's provisions for their defence. This must also extend to the wider countryside, so that the relevance of the protected area series as a whole is kept under surveillance. If the SSSI measures prove inadequate or losses in the wider countryside continue unacceptably, the nature conservation movement will press for further expansion of the protected area series or new and stronger legislative measures.

15.2.7 Site acquisition is only the first part of protection: the second is management to maintain the nature conservation interest, which requires a substantial and continuing resource input. A separate management programme needs developing, as follows:—

15.2.7.1 Prepare management plans for all nature reserves, and eventually for all categories of protected area. The format of the NNR Management Plan should be the longer-term goal, but short interim plans should be used when other priorities press heavily. Plans should include projected resource costs. A management review should also be launched, dealing with the needs of whole suites of reserves according to ecosystem type.

15.2.7.2 Produce management manuals and handbooks for all main ecosystem types, with booklets/leaflets for more specialised manipulation of communities and species and information notes as relevant management research projects are completed.

15.2.7.3 Establish systematic recording schemes for all reserves (within their management plans), to provide an inventory of environmental and biological attributes of each and to monitor these site features and activities and events on the reserves. Information should be published as a reserve handbook at an appropriate stage. Each reserve should also have a descriptive leaflet.

15.2.7.4 Develop research programmes (linked with 15.5) to take account of further information and methodological needs under 15.2.7.1 and 15.2.7.2, and feed back results accordingly.

15.2.7.5 Review wardening needs for reserves as a whole, and include in resource requirements. The high cost of wardening necessitates examination of possibilities for sharing manpower, equipment and information between different parties with adjacent reserves and requires the increasing use of both voluntary assistance and job creation schemes supported by government funds.

15.2.8 As part of the review of management, policy on public access to and use of reserves should be more specifically rationalised between parties according to the following considerations:—

15.2.8.1 Apply the general principle of allowing or encouraging maximum visitor use compatible with maintenance of the nature conservation interest on those reserves set up and managed from public or membership funds.

15.2.8.2 Continue to develop some reserves (or parts of them) in areas of high public pressure as educational sites with suitable facilities, e.g. nature trails, guided tours, interpretative centres, literature and maps. **Manage reserves important for fragile habitats and sensitive species, or**

for **wilderness character, to protect these attributes.** On still other reserves there should be neither restriction nor invitation as regards visitor access, and public pressure should be allowed to reach its own level, as determined by the motivation of people interested to seek out nature in their own way. The use of reserves should be monitored, and feed-back obtained on public views about them.

15.2.8.3 **Encourage the scientific use of reserves (at least NNRs) and support research projects where possible.** The development of such work links with 15.5 (Research — especially 15.5.3), needs for the study of management problems (15.2.7.4) and, in the setting-up and use of Biosphere Reserves, with 15.8 (International conservation).

15.3   **Theme 2: Conservation of nature in the wider environment**
15.3.1 The national resource of nature in the 90 + % (at present 93%) of Britain outside protected areas is greatly at risk, for the recent scale and rate of damage and loss are a most worrying portent. In the arable 'prairies', especially in eastern England, wildlife and its habitat are already reduced to pathetic remnants outside reserves and SSSIs. If trends continue unabated there is a real prospect that this state of affairs will become increasingly widespread in other districts. And, although the extent of mountain, moorland and peat bog in the upland districts remains large, this too will be subjected to continuing attrition through afforestation, reclamation, draining, peat-winning and other activities. Destruction of the more vulnerable geological features and landforms will also become increasingly serious. This largely unprotected wider environment contains the greater part of our national capital of nature and it is indispensable, especially as it represents the most accessible and available part of nature to most people. Its conservation must continue to be achieved largely through the contributions of other land and natural resource users, especially the owners and occupiers. Targets here can hardly be explicit, however, and the approach should be the open-ended one of seeking to achieve as much as possible through the promotion of sympathetic attitudes and actions amongst those concerned. Increased effort will be made to convey to other parties the great importance attached to conservation in the wider countryside and to redress the imbalance created by the post-1981 emphasis on SSSIs. The following will be the main approaches:—

15.3.2 **Persuade government to amend rural policies in ways which reduce their damaging effects on nature, and encourage socio-economic activities supportive of environmental conservation.** The conservation bodies should recruit agricultural, forestry and economic expertise to examine the socio-economic arguments which underpin present policies for agriculture and forestry, and to recommend changes meeting both national and social

Tees valley

objectives whilst giving substantial improvements to the conservation of wildlife and physical features. These alternatives will take due account of the need to maintain viable rural communities through remuneration and employment, and especially of the feasibility of directing existing public subsidies to a wider range of objectives and activities than are presently supported. Liaison with individual Departments of State, governmental agencies and public utilities will seek acceptance of these proposals and also clear statements of intention to pay regard to the needs of nature conservation. The earlier concept of a National Land-use Strategy has attracted little support and will not be pursued further. There is, nevertheless, great need for central integration of land-use policies in a way that recognises the problems and requirements of nature conservation.

15.3.3 Strengthen liaison with local authorities with a view to obtaining further commitment to the objectives of nature conservation. Improvements in appropriate contacts and inputs will be planned, especially over advisory and information support to formal planning, conservation of National Parks, AONBs, Heritage Coasts and National Scenic Areas, urban conservation and creation of new habitats, surveys and data collection, and education and public relations. Collaborative projects on integrated policies for rural areas, involving redirection of public funds for alternative activities (such as the Peak District project) will be supported. Special efforts will be made to obtain a more positive response from those authorities whose interest in nature conservation has previously been weak.

15.3.4 Develop a rationale for nature conservation as a socially necessary activity, including its relevance to spiritual, leisure and recreational needs and to employment. The needs of wardening, of the management of land, habitats and species and of informing, guiding and otherwise catering for the public enjoyment of nature provide considerable job opportunities which have to be quantified. This is especially important in rural areas where unemployment is serious and nature conservation tends to be viewed as inhibitory to job creation.

15.3.5 Produce detailed statements of problems and proposed policies for each of the main land and natural resource use interests. These will follow the style of NCC's **Nature conservation and agriculture.** They will be preceded by discussions with the interests concerned,

who will be invited to state their intentions for paying regard to nature conservation. The conservation side will identify ways of working with these interests in trying to meet its objectives. Ways will also be sought of enhancing the advisory input to other land-users and understanding their needs, so that they can improve the integration of nature conservation with their primary objectives. These will include support for FWAG and development of comparable groups for other interests besides farming and forestry if this seems desirable.

15.3.6 Develop a monitoring programme to measure changes to wildlife and physical features in the wider environment, especially in relation to human impact; and maintain parallel surveillance of environmental policies (e.g. planning, green belt and urban activities, and fiscal measures) which have either beneficial or adverse effects. Associated aims should be to develop a predictive and analytical capacity for anticipating and evaluating future trends in land and natural resource uses, and to maintain awareness of technical changes and other developments which may impinge beneficially or adversely on nature conservation, e.g. advances in biological control of agricultural and forestry pest organisms. The case for adopting formal Environmental Impact Statements for development projects in Britain will be carefully examined.

15.3.7 Press for stronger representation of nature conservation interests within relevant official and unofficial bodies, both by appropriate memberships of councils and committees and through staff expertise. The NCC and NGOs should both aim to strengthen their own internal scientific advisory and representational capacity in parallel ways, and they should expand their range of technical competence into neglected areas.

15.4   **Theme 3: Marine nature conservation**
15.4.1 Marine ecosystems are the Cinderella of nature conservation in Britain. No measures for taking conservation action below low tide level existed until the 1981 Act provided for the creation of Marine Nature Reserves. There is no marine sublittoral equivalent to the SSSI, and conservation in the wider marine environment is limited to government and international fisheries policies and pollution control legislation agreements. Even the attempts by NCC to establish the first MNR have been beset by problems, largely the difficulty of making byelaws as required under the Act. About 30% of the intertidal (littoral) zone of Britain

has now been surveyed, but the much more difficult survey of the shallow coastal waters (sublittoral) — which must be carried out by diving — has only just begun. Such survey is necessary to comprehend the national range of variation in marine ecosystems, and hence to identify the important sites deserving protection. The following programme is therefore proposed:—

15.4.2 Launch immediately a Marine Nature Conservation Review to identify prospective MNRs (key sites) and other sites of regional importance. It will be necessary first to secure the appropriate resources for the surveys involved and to enlist help from the Marine Conservation Society.

15.4.3 Vigorously pursue negotiations for establishing the first MNR and, if these fail, press government to make its legislation succeed. If, after this, the existing measures prove unworkable, new and more satisfactory legislation must be urgently sought.

15.4.4 Promote nature conservation in the wider marine environment outside statutory sites, by the following means:—

15.4.4.1 selective monitoring programmes, designed to detect ecological change in the littoral and sublittoral zones, at sample locations round the coast;

15.4.4.2 seeking beneficial modification of government and EEC policies which adversely affect marine nature conservation interests; these include especially fisheries policies, but also the indirect effects of relevant economic and fiscal policies;

15.4.4.3 giving greater attention to implementation of the Control of Pollution Act 1974 and of other legislation and international agreements relating to marine pollution. It is especially important to avoid pollution within the key sites for marine nature conservation.

Cup-coral, *Leptopsammia pruvoti*

Burnt Island, St. Agnes, Scilly

15.5   Theme 4: Research and dissemination of technical information

15.5.1 Nature conservation practice depends on the scientific application of technical knowledge obtained by study of the phenomena of nature, including descriptive data on the character, distribution and abundance of plant and animal communities and species and geological and physiographic features; the measurement of the rate and scale of changes in these; cause-effect relationships between organisms and environmental influences (including the causes of change) and the dynamics of both biological and physical processes and systems. Past work has provided a large body of information on all these subjects but it is never sufficient to meet more than a small proportion of the questions which conservationists have to answer in both specific and general cases; and so the need for further study presses heavily and continuously. There are, accordingly, two primary needs — the first being to enlarge this essential information base through new research and the second to make the best possible use of the information existing at any one time.

15.5.2 Future research and information requirements should be systematically analysed and set out in the form of costed programmes, under the main categories below:—

15.5.2.1 Countrywide survey of all biological and physical features to provide the scientific background knowledge for evaluation, to identify the best sites for the protected area series, the species most in need of conservation measures, the management needs and the most urgent problems in the wider environment. The priority will be to complete survey of physical features, vegetation and the more closely studied groups of plants and animals. Adequate survey of many lower plant and invertebrate groups is a long-term objective.

15.5.2.2 Monitoring to detect and measure change in biological and physical features, and thus to diagnose conservation problems, order priorities for action and adjust relevant policies. Accurate, up-to-date knowledge of change, especially to assess damage and loss, has to underpin discussion of other land and natural resource use policies and the effectiveness of legislation. Monitoring could be limitless and it is therefore necessary to restrict it to situations where change is anticipated or has actually begun. The 1981 Act requires that the schedules of specially protected wild plants and animals be reviewed every five years, and suitable amendments made. Since monitoring is repeated survey, it is important that, whenever possible, initial surveys (i.e. under 15.5.2.1) should be conducted in a standardised and repeatable manner.

15.5.2.3 Ecological studies to elucidate cause-effect relationships between natural phenomena and controlling

Research on peat bog

90

environmental factors, especially when change is found but the causes are uncertain or when interacting factors make causal interpretation difficult. These studies must take account of normal fluctuations in species' populations so that new and longer-term trends can be detected or confirmed. They should also include work on relevant processes such as those involved in pollution effects, the analysis of complex systems of relationships, and studies of important wildlife species (especially endangered species). The insights of ecological research are especially necessary to **management,** in providing knowledge to guide desired manipulation of ecosystems and species. This applies not only to reserves, but to integration of nature conservation with other land-uses in the wider environment, through modification of farming and silvicultural practices, and to creative conservation. Such knowledge is also essential for informed debate of controversial issues over human impacts.

15.5.2.4 Other miscellaneous research needs which do not easily fall under one heading, e.g. development of new techniques, socio-economic studies and data-handling systems. Environmental impact assessment will require research, and its needs should be considered here.

15.5.3 The need for further research in all these fields is very great and requires careful balance, with a strict ordering of priorities. **The conservation bodies should seek ways of increasing the amount of supporting research, through a concerted approach,** as follows:—

15.5.3.1 **Expand survey and monitoring through voluntary assistance within the NGOs, along established lines, e.g. species mapping and site recording, with scheme organisers.** Urge government to accept recording of wildlife and human impacts as part of national environmental resource stock-taking (cf. geological and soil survey and climatological recording).

15.5.3.2 **Promote applied and strategic ecological research through a suitable approach to NERC (and its grant-aid policy), the universities, British Ecological Society and Royal Society.** Identify the existing distribution of research activity, gaps in knowledge and major conservation needs, and relevant themes for new work. Reciprocate by offering reserves as study areas, help from wardens, use of available data, maps and photographs, etc.

15.5.3.3 **Press for the 'developer pays' principle to be more firmly applied over various kinds of research** by departments

and non-governmental bodies whose interests have damaging effects on nature, i.e. agriculture, fisheries, forestry, industry and water, energy and mineral use. Urge these parties also to take a positive interest in management research.

15.5.3.4 **Tackle the 'compartmental' problem in the management of ecological research related to the last two items.** This arises when different bodies have a common but divergent interest in the same topic and approach it independently and in different ways. Sometimes, also, a problem clearly falls to the remit of one interest, but they are reluctant to deal with it. In such cases, shared responsibility for research planning and priority-setting, if not for actual collaborative work, is needed.

15.5.4 To make the best use of existing information, the conservation bodies should analyse their technical data needs and develop appropriate retrieval systems. Expertise on computing hardware and software should be shared and data pooled as far as possible. Other techniques such as ground and air photography, digitised cartography and the use of satellite imagery in mapping and monitoring should be exploited according to their usefulness. Stores and collections of data, maps, photographs and other relevant material should be catalogued and indexed within a single reference system which users can draw upon, subject to normal confidentiality, according to their needs. NCC data on monitoring of special sites and the wider countryside should be part of the information pool. A suitable means of maintaining awareness of new developments and advising on relevant application of appropriate techniques should be sought.

15.5.5 There should be an increased translation of scientific information, both extant and new, into technical papers, reviews, management prescriptions and guidance, books and other popular publications on nature conservation. This should link with the publicity and educational programmes and seek improved presentation and dissemination of results. It should identify gaps in the information field and provide for their filling, by attaching greater importance to this publication as the last and essential phase of research and development. Commissioned research should make greater provision within the contracts for the publication of the results.

15.6   Theme 5: Publicity and education

15.6.1 These are among the most vital activities, for nature conservation will succeed in direct relation to people's knowledge and concern about it. Publicity and education are regarded by many as two different matters, but they shade gradually into each other and are here treated together. Education about nature is a desirable cultural goal, in enriching the lives of people and providing fulfilling ways of using their leisure time through contact with nature. It increases understanding of and concern for nature conservation within society generally and, still more importantly, amongst the politicians, administrators and other land and natural resource users who collectively exert so much influence over the use of our natural environment. There is a particular need to inform policy makers, resource managers and decision takers about nature conservation. Knowledge of ecological principles, resource management issues and environmental affairs generally is also part of a liberal education which helps to give people a better understanding of their world and an increased regard for it. A great deal of excellent work has already been done across the whole field, but much more is needed. The following approaches are to be adopted:—

15.6.2 Expand the commitment, including resource support, to publicity to increase the production of material for presenting the nature conservation message and the capacity for lobbying and promotional action. The level of professional public relations support should be increased in planning the future approach. Media support should be sought in a more organised way, leading to a more positive rather than reactive approach to television and other media. Museums, public libraries and other educational institutions should be encouraged to increase their presentation of material on environmental conservation. The conservation bodies should help by providing more material for use through these channels. Some botanical and zoological gardens already emphasise the conservation needs of flora and fauna and their own relevance to this, and others could follow suit. Urban nature conservation has an important role here, in bringing a wider group of people into contact with wildlife. More field and interpretative centres should be established and such places should be better supplied with books, leaflets and

Ynyslas Information Centre, Dyfi NNR

other literature on the local natural history and nature conservation. New editions of the Ordnance Survey tourist maps could incorporate additional wildlife information, such as the boundaries of nature reserves and location of field and interpretative centres.

15.6.3 Organise workshops and seminars to analyse and discuss the communication of conservation and technical issues, including training courses and other methods, and the cost-effectiveness of the different approaches. To underpin the whole approach, the philosophy and rationale of nature conservation need better definition and presentation; and the style of address appropriate to particular audiences needs careful thought. Any interested party, and especially the individual, should be able to see quite clearly how he or she can become involved and contribute to the movement. A popular presentation of this document is desirable, and also one which spells out the need for public participation and makes a clarion-call appeal to the nation as a whole, aiming to increase the acceptance of nature conservation through the direct involvement of more and more people.

15.6.4 Commit the nature conservation movement to supporting and encouraging environmental education in all possible ways, and within this general goal ensure that the teaching of ecology and natural resource conservation (including wildlife and physical features) receives due attention. The task of changing educational programmes will not be easy at any level; a great number of people are involved in education and the present pressures on them are considerable. Only by winning the sympathy of educational-ists, influencing the training of future teachers and encouraging policy decisions which will benefit environmental education can the situation be improved. The Council for Environmental Education (CEE), which represents both educational and conservation organisations, provides the best forum for such developments. It is vital that environmental education should be understood and encouraged by the education policy-makers at national and local levels and within higher education as well as the school and non-formal sectors. A strategy needs to be developed by CEE, with support from conservationists, which aims at substantial improvement in the quantity and quality of environmental education.

15.6.5 Help educationalists to improve environmental education within their own areas of interest. For schools all possible support should be given to those trying to influence the school curriculum and examinations beneficially. This involves teaching all children a wide range of subjects by using the local environment as a medium for learning and encouraging them to understand and care for their surroundings. Advice on nature conservation, production of teaching materials and provision of wildlife areas for educational use encourage teachers to become involved with environmental education. At the further education and university levels all those whose future work is likely to affect the environment should be made aware of conservation issues and solutions. There are already moves to promote nature conservation instruction in agricultural colleges, but in many disciplines, for example engineering, sociology, politics and economics, there is still virtually no environmental education. And despite an increase in various university courses in the subject, it is not yet possible to obtain a first degree in conservation. Within the non-formal sector some imaginative schemes for increasing environmental interest within youth clubs have begun; these need encouragement and greatly increased financial support.

15.7 **Theme 6: Legislation for nature conservation**

15.7.1 Nature conservation legislation has been discussed under 4.4, 11.3, 12.3 and 15.4. The provisions affecting site safeguard (i.e. both habitats and species) have been dealt with under 15.2 but those relating to the wider environment are primarily concerned with species protection, and these are considered below. Nature conservation is highly dependent upon relevant law and its effectiveness, and it is essential to monitor this closely. All the nature conservation legislation will be kept under close surveillance and reviewed periodically, with the aim of identifying weaknesses and seeking appropriate remedy, if necessary by pressing for new legislation. Other existing and proposed legislation which either affects or might affect nature conservation interests, either adversely or beneficially, will also be monitored. Species legislation is countrywide law protecting wild flora and fauna against unauthorised taking and killing; it will be supported by the following action:—

15.7.2 Operate the licensing procedures for permitted exclusions in taking/killing of flora and fauna, and act or advise on other issues arising under the 1981 Act. These include policy on licence quotas, *ad hoc* changes in schedule listings of species according to alteration in status, hard-weather bans on wildfowling and other matters dealt with by orders at the discretion of the Secretary of State. This process relies on technical advice supplied by biologists and related to research programmes under 15.5.

15.7.3 Review every five years the schedules of species of wild animals and plants protected under the 1981 Act. This is a statutory requirement and depends on close monitoring of the status of all the rarer species of vertebrate, the best known invertebrate groups and the flowering plants and ferns. Some of these are covered by the British Red Data Books listing vulnerable and endangered species, but election to the special schedules also depends on criteria other than rarity, such as attractiveness and proneness to collecting.

15.7.4 Extend the Red Data Book treatment of threatened wildlife to other taxonomic groups of plants and animals, so that other species in need of special protection can be clearly identified. This relates to the survey and monitoring programmes of 15.5.2, including the need for better information on neglected groups.

15.7.5 Improve enforcement of the law, especially in regard to illegal taking and killing of birds of prey and egg collecting, killing of badgers and collecting of rare insects and plants. While there have been considerable improvements in recent years, illegal killing of birds of prey is still widespread and the taking of their young into captivity has substantially increased. Collecting of eggs and specially

protected wildlife continues, and orchids are especially at risk. Increased resources are needed if enforcement is to become properly effective: it has greatly relied on voluntary and spare-time efforts in the past, and Britain has no official enforcement agency akin to the US Fish and Wildlife Service.

15.7.6 Increase publicity to promote greater awareness of wildlife protection laws. The community at large needs to be better informed about the laws on species protection. School children should be taught about such matters. And, since enforcement usually involves the police, they should also be instructed as a matter of course. Much of the problem, however, rests with people who know the law perfectly well but choose to break it. The greater need here is to promote a climate of opinion which will make breaking of the wildlife laws carry a greater social stigma. Beyond this, the modern attitudes to collecting of certain plants and animals as an activity which should now be restricted to approved scientific purpose should be encouraged to spread to all wildlife, so that protection does not depend on the sanction of law. This work is an integral part of publicity and education (15.6).

15.7.7 Meet obligations under international legislation. This consists especially of licensing and enforcement under the Endangered Species (Import and Export) Act 1976, dealing with trade in endangered plants and animals. The need to react to the EEC Directives affecting nature conservation (e.g. bird habitats) is dealt with under the next theme.

Abernethy Forest SSSI

Spring gentian

15.8   Theme 7: International nature conservation

15.8.1 The international role of nature conservation is increasingly important. The contribution from the nature conservation bodies should be better co-ordinated and strengthened, in regard both to the further development of policy overseas and to the implementation of policy in this country. Continued support should be given to the development and implementation of international conventions for nature conservation, such as the Ramsar (wetland conservation), Berne (threatened species and their habitats), Bonn (migratory species) and Washington (CITES — trade in endangered species) Conventions, and programmes such as the United Nations Environment Programme and the European network of biogenetic reserves, particularly in the identification of sites, habitats and species requiring protection through them. Commitment to measures for supporting international research projects, such as through UNESCO Biosphere Reserves, should be strengthened, by developing study programmes and increasing the number of such reserves. The UK government has agreed to sign the World Heritage Convention.

15.8.2 The close links with the Council of Europe and its committees dealing with nature conservation should be maintained, and the relationship with the European Commission and its Directorates General dealing with activities which impinge on nature conservation should be strengthened. The aim is to ensure that nature conservation interests continue to be accommodated in the affairs of the Council of Europe and are better placed in the policies and programmes of the EEC. The Common Agricultural Policy, in particular, is having a very strong impact on nature conservation throughout the EEC, and it is important to the achievement of the overall objective (15.1) that some of its damaging effects be reduced or removed by suitable amendment. It is also crucial that the existing provisions for promoting environmental concerns within EEC legislation are interpreted in the UK in ways which are more favourable to nature conservation than in the past. The EEC could also become a more significant source of funding for research on projects relevant to nature conservation.

15.8.3 The NC supported IUCN from 1949 onwards and later, with the Countryside Commissions, represented the UK government in membership. Over the years IUCN has become a powerful voice in international nature conservation, most notably in its co-sponsorship of the World Conservation Strategy. NCC will continue to provide the Chair and Secretariat for the UK Committee for IUCN, which is the focus for the discussion of IUCN affairs and the development of IUCN policies in

White-fronted geese

95

Britain. The IUCN Conservation Plan will be particularly relevant to this.

15.8.4 NCC should aim to have greater influence in advising government on the nature conservation significance of its overseas aid policies and programmes, especially where there are development proposals in areas important for wildlife and physical features. In particular, the conservation movement should seek to influence government activities in respect of UK dependencies, both with regard to integrating environmental safeguards in development projects funded by government and in the implementation of international wildlife conventions, including those establishing networks of protected areas. NCC should co-ordinate this advice. Influence should also be exerted through such channels as OECD, the EEC and other international bodies through which UK aid funds are channelled.

15.8.5 The contribution to international evaluation of nature conservation interest and problems should be maintained, as for example by supporting the work in monitoring the status of the world's animal and plant species undertaken by IUCN's Conservation Monitoring Centre. Britain should obtain an independent appraisal of the international importance of its biological and physical features by overseas scientists and conservationists, so that its nature conservation priorities can take account of especially valued features. This is particularly important since government has a statutory duty under international agreements to protect them.

15.8.6 Britain must continue to exchange information, experience and ideas with the international community of nature conservationists. Co-operation over common problems should be further developed, for example on acid deposition, migratory species and trade in protected wildlife, and this should include research inputs in collaboration with scientists in other countries (as has successfully been done for pesticide problems).

15.8.7 Much of the international work will have to be done by NCC and the larger NGOs (RSPB, RSNC and WWF), but NGO involvement should be increased. NCC must as far as possible maintain its independent voice on international matters, as it does on domestic issues (4.1). This will include urging government when necessary to implement its obligations under international conventions and other measures.

15.9   **Theme 8: Creative conservation**
15.9.1 Creative conservation seeks to enlarge the resource of nature by recreating habitats and communities or reintroducing species lost through human impact. Opportunities occur, especially through abandonment of mineral workings, for natural processes of plant and animal colonisation to restore semi-natural communities. These can be

Ford Green Hall nature reserve, Stoke

accelerated and diversified by deliberate manipulation of physical conditions and species and applied to land available or acquired for the purpose. Some habitats resulting from long-term geological processes cannot be re-created, for example limestone pavements, but some physiographic processes such as coastal sedimentation can be manipulated, given the necessary conditions and resources. Semi-natural ecosystems such as lowland grasslands and broad-leaved woodlands are amenable to this kind of re-creation, though it may be difficult or even impossible to ensure that they contain the full species complement of the original types. Species reintroductions can be difficult, but success depends especially on adequate management insight provided by autecological studies. A programme for a series of projects on recreation of habitats and communities and reintroduction of species should be constructed, with underpinning by the following main elements:—

15.9.2 Acquire precise knowledge of the full floristic, faunistic and habitat composition of the types of ecosystem which it is desired to re-create (refers to primary survey of existing types — 15.5.2.1).

15.9.3 Obtain adequate ecological knowledge of the needs and behaviour of the species and communities it is proposed to re-establish, in relation to controlling environmental conditions (refers to ecological and autecological research in 15.5.2.3 and production of management handbooks and manuals in 15.2.7.2).

15.9.4 Discuss the public relations aspects (including within the nature conservation movement itself) of proposals which may be controversial, especially those involving the introduction, reintroduction, translocation and restocking of species.

15.9.5 Use plant propagation and animal captive breeding techniques already well-tried, to support survival and reintroduction work.

15.9.6 Ensure the availability of the technical skills and mechanical equipment needed to manipulate physical conditions, as necessary, including landform, soil conditions, drainage and water-table.

15.9.7 Support government in its obligations to control the introduction of alien species and seek, where desirable and possible, to reintroduce species that have recently become extinct.

15.9.8 Seek and exploit favourable, preferably low-cost, opportunities for habitat re-creation and species reintroduction through the co-operation of sympathetic landowners, both corporate and individual, and publicise successful results. Such opportunities should be considered first, but at some stage it will be desirable increasingly to acquire land specially for the purpose.

15.9.9 Habitats which it is important and feasible to re-establish include estuarine saltmarsh, broad-leaved native woodland and scrub, meadow (neutral) grassland, mixed grass-heath, lowland lake and pond hydroseres, lowland rich and poor fen and lowland raised mire.

15.9.10 Some habitats are difficult to re-create except on a very small scale; they include calcareous grassland (downland), acidic heathland, bryophyte and lichen communities of western woods, river communities and montane vegetation in general. Much more research is thus needed on these difficult types.

15.9.11 It is often assumed that the abandonment of farming, including hill grazing, would be bad for nature conservation. In some situations it might actually be the best thing that could happen from a wildlife viewpoint. This is not to advocate such abandonment, but to be ready to react if this should chance to happen. At least the matter should be tested by acquiring a range of different types of farmland as experimental areas and allowing them to revert to a state of nature, with careful monitoring of the changes. Small exclosure plots on moorland give only a limited idea of vegetational change, and larger areas would be needed to observe the effects on animal populations.

15.9.12 Both foresters and nature conservationists should accept the challenge of the oft-repeated assertion that the extensive new coniferous forests in upland and heathland areas offer great opportunities for wildlife conservation in future. It will be necessary to find out how existing silvicultural practice should be modified to exploit these opportunities meaningfully. Species composition, thinning and felling regimes, ground treatment and management of open ground habitats and open waters need examination. Realisation of such opportunities will be closely related to willingness to forgo maximisation of crop yield and to the forestry industry's preparedness to bear this within a broadened conception of forestry objectives in Britain. It has, after all, been accepted that a lower than standard test rate of discount should be allowed for assessment of returns on forestry, because of its social value in rural areas, including its value for amenity and recreation.

15.9.13 Habitat re-creation is especially relevant to urban nature conservation, in the utilisation of opportunities provided by waste ground of various kinds and other areas such as parks and even gardens. This will depend especially on local authorities' willingness and initiative, but there are already many striking examples to follow, and voluntary help is usually the least of the problems. Information on techniques and suitable species is needed, but the precise objectives can be less exacting than in trying to re-create semi-natural ecosystems in the countryside. Each urban wildlife group should define its own programme and set objectives according to local perception of need and situation.

15.9.14 The Countryside Commission has taken important initiatives in this field, including its experimental farm projects. Some local authorities are also developing valuable projects. The scope for this creative conservation is almost limitless, though it can only be carried out on a small scale for some time to come. It could perhaps snowball in the more densely populated districts, and the necessary ingredients for carrying it forward are — besides technical knowledge — boldness, determination and imagination.

15.10   Theme 9: Resources for nature conservation

15.10.1 The future success of the nature conservation movement will depend greatly on both its effective use of available money and manpower and its ability to enlarge these resources. Each of the previous eight main elements of strategy must be further analysed in depth in developing future programmes, and they must be costed in both manpower and money. The planning process will take careful account of the distribution of effort (15.11) between the various contributing organisations, notably NCC and the NGOs, but including commitments by other bodies, to optimise the use of these resources. NCC grant-aid policy to the NGOs will be further reviewed, in regard to site acquisition, site and other practical management, and administrative support. There will be an analysis of the resource gaps between the targets achievable with the present level of resources and those identified in the programmes as additionally necessary to achieve desirable targets.

15.10.2 The nature conservation movement must do what it can to help itself. It will be helpful for NGOs to review their activities for fund-raising from non-governmental sources, including public and individual appeals, sponsorship, sales and, above all, further membership drives. This will be closely related to public relations programmes under 15.6. There is a proper reluctance to charge for the use of nature, but the issue should be appraised to see whether payment for facilities and materials would be an acceptable option, or under what circumstances charging would be valid. There are already precedents, such as charging for access to nature reserves by non-members and for the use of car parks. The practice of the US Nature Conservancy (a private organisation) of selling off nature reserves under restrictive covenants should also be carefully examined in the British context, by both NCC and NGOs.

15.10.3 There remains the reality that the core of financial support for nature conservation will have to continue to come from the public purse, either centrally

Kirkby Moor nature reserve

from the Treasury or locally through rates. And while every effort must be made to persuade local authorities to promote nature conservation and to include it as a service to the community through rates, it is also inescapable that the allocation of taxpayers' money through central government Grant-in-Aid will remain the most crucial element in this public funding. NCC is almost wholly dependent on such finance, and so therefore is its ability to support the voluntary sector through its grant function. The fundamental task is thus to persuade government to allocate more money to nature conservation, and especially to increase aid to the voluntary sector.

15.10.4 The reserve acquisition programme should continue to be shared between NCC and the NGOs, with the latter taking as much of the load as possible, in accordance with central policy over redistribution of public funds to the private sector. The cost of meeting section 28 and 29 procedures on threatened SSSIs under the 1981 Act should continue to be the separate responsibility of DoE, acting through NCC, and government has declared its commitment to such funding of SSSI safeguard. It will, however, be necessary for NCC to maintain a separate and positive (as distinct from reactive) programme for acquisition of sites of National Nature Reserve quality, especially by utilising low-cost opportunities. NGOs will also acquire such top grade sites, but are not limited to them in establishing reserves.

15.10.5 Much has already been done to obtain government financial assistance by less direct approaches, notably the use of fiscal measures and incentives for nature conservation, and these should be reviewed periodically. The case for redistributing public subsidies to agriculture for a wider range of rural activities, including to farmers for nature conservation management, must continue to be pressed vigorously. The 'developer pays' principle for funding of relevant research and restoration must be urged upon both government departments and private enterprises which create nature conservation problems. Above all, there must be a concerted effort to convey to government the triviality of its present recognition of nature conservation in financial terms when this is set against the national wealth (Figure 11). Even within the field of cultural purpose, nature conservation fares badly, with a 1984/1985 budget of £14 · 4 million compared with £29 · 36 million for the Sports Council and £100 million for the Arts Council. There is scant acceptance in this of either the value or the irreplaceability of the resource of nature as a national asset and heritage. The importance of nature to science, as a biogenetic resource, to the use of leisure time, to both mental and physical health and to the overall quality of human existence and civilisation deserves a much more commensurate share of the public purse than it now receives. There is good evidence that the public itself wants this, for example in a MORI public opinion poll conducted for the UK Conservation and Development Programme. The nature conservation bodies should continue to urge that this country should set a better example by making much more adequate provision for this key area of environmental policy.

15.10.6 Manpower largely depends on finance, but in the public sector it is also separately subject to the constraint of

Dolebury Warren

government policy. It must be used with maximum efficiency by the conservation bodies. The nature conservation movement has also to demonstrate more effectively its potential for job creation, especially in districts with serious unemployment problems. Manpower Services Commission schemes are already being used by both NGOs and NCC to considerable mutual benefit, in having valuable conservation work done and temporary employment and training provided. A more definitive set of proposals should be drawn up, identifying the overall scope for such work opportunities across all the main elements of the strategy.

15.10.7 Finally, the nature conservation bodies should, with the help of economic and other technical advisers, pay still closer attention to the economic, financial and manpower arguments which are adduced to justify the present policy framework in regard to the balance between the various land and resource use elements in the overall national interest. They should endeavour to add the arguments for their own interest in similar fashion, within the public debate on these matters.

15.11   **Theme 10: The distribution of effort**

15.11.1 This document is a statement of intent by those responsible for promoting nature conservation. While primarily conceived as a package to guide future action by those bodies whose main function this is, it is also addressed to all parties able to contribute to the nation's total programme for nature conservation. An important part of strategy is therefore to answer the question 'Who does what?' by determining the relationships and apportioning the contributions between the various parties concerned. The more detailed planning of programmes must then work out how and where all interested parties can actually contribute.

15.11.2 The conservation bodies should achieve closer integration, defining a collective approach, at both policy and operation levels, and distributing individual efforts according to respective strengths and responsibilities. Action programmes (including corporate plans) should be co-ordinated and consultation mechanisms devised: the latter might include both standing and *ad hoc* liaison groups or 'think tanks' at regional and national levels, for example on the reserve acquisition programme, on research requirements, and on socio-economic problems and nature conservation. The nature conservation bodies should urgently examine, with the two Countryside Commissions and the two

National Trusts, ways of developing a more satisfactory functional interface between wildlife and geological conservation on the one hand and scenic and countryside amenity conservation on the other. Common objectives and means of establishing more mutually supporting relationships should be identified.

15.11.3 NCC has statutory duties, including responsibility for advising ministers and accounting to parliament in various ways. It also has a remit and an expertise (including scientific competence) which span the whole field of nature conservation, so that it is ideally placed to give leadership to the whole movement. The NGOs have a greater political freedom as a lobby and a larger potential capacity for action in various fields — survey, management, education and publicity. The respective strengths of the partners must be utilised. While the Rayner scrutiny of NCC concluded that little of the organisation's functions could be privatised, nevertheless, NCC could increasingly become the avenue for distributing funds for conservation to the NGOs. The partners must therefore maintain a system of operation which achieves the optimum results according to whatever balance of support is imposed by government at any one time. There must, however, be greater mutual confidence and trust than in the past.

15.11.4 The conservation movement should examine and promote ways of increasing its internal support by mobilising and focusing the very considerable body of public interest in nature which is diffused through the community. Ways should be sought to integrate nature conservation as cause for concern within the mainstream social, cultural and economic life of the nation. While this document necessarily tends to take a centralised view, it recognises the importance of the populist aspect of the subject and the need for a democratic approach. The aim should be to complement the centralised approach with one which is decentralised and community-based, as are some of the recent local initiatives within the conservation movement.

15.11.5 The conservation bodies should also try to obtain statements of intended contributions from other parties who have a duty to take account of nature conservation in the pursuit of their primary interests, including government departments and agencies, public utilities and local authorities, and from private interests who have a moral responsibility to do so (15.3).

16

The courage of conviction

16.1 Prescriptions for ways of enhancing the total nature conservation effort have been made. Some are undeniable and urgent, others tentative and exploratory. Most will be likely to need more people and more money if appreciable improvements are to be achieved. But, whatever the measures and the resources to implement them, the results will also depend on the skill, vigour and tact with which the various approaches are made. Nature conservation has in the past sometimes conducted its business on too apologetic and timid a note. Such a tendency to submissive posture is a recipe for retaining a low peck-order position in the league of land and resource use interests. If nature conservation is to gain the acceptance it deserves as a relevant concern for the whole of society, its practitioners all have to behave as though it really matters. Conservationists must argue their interests and their cases with a firmness and conviction which stem from a visible belief in and commitment to the things they talk about. This is not to advocate aggressiveness and exaggeration, but the playing of a hard yet clean game for our side. There are management and training aspects to be considered here, but these will count for little if the right messages do not come from the top. And for all those who affirm the importance of nature conservation, the challenge will be to turn opportunity and intention into achievement. Posterity will judge all of us by deeds and not words.

Annex 1

1:1 Categories of protected area for nature conservation

The total area of land protected for nature conservation in some way is approximately 1,679,500 hectares, equivalent to about 7% of the land surface of Britain. In addition, apart from their SSSI designated landholdings, the National Trust and the National Trust for Scotland hold between them more than 120,000 hectares which is of nature conservation interest.

Commands 7122 (England and Wales) and 7184 (Scotland) contained proposals for 124 biological National Nature Reserves. Of these 57 are now wholly or in part NNRs and 19 others are now reserves of some kind including seven National Trust properties.

Only a handful of these sites are no longer judged to be of sufficient interest to merit SSSI status. However it is important to note that in many cases the size of a site now protected in some way is considerably smaller than that originally proposed as a reserve. For example:

	Proposed reserve (hectares)	Area protected (hectares)
Wye and Crundale Downs	600	132
Blean Woods	770	220

A Nature Conservation Review identified 735 biological sites of national importance to nature conservation in Britain. Another 73 such key sites have subsequently been added to this list. Almost all of the current NNRs are key sites and the remaining unprotected NCR sites will provide the 'shopping list' for further biological NNR acquisitions.

The Report of the Geological sub-Committee of the Nature Reserves Investigation Committee (1945) proposed 390 'geological reserves' in various categories. Of these, 346 are now geological SSSIs. The Geological Conservation Review at present nearing completion has identified approximately 1,500 sites of national geological importance, two-thirds of which are already SSSI.

The number of marine sites so far identified as meriting reserve status is 26, of which seven have been selected to be actively promoted as proposed Marine Nature Reserves. Only when a Marine Nature Conservation Review, parallel to the other two, has been completed will it be possible to say how many additional sites may be considered of national importance and worthy of protection as MNRS.

1:5 Loss of neutral grassland

Neutral grassland was described by Tansley (1939) as semi-natural grassland on fertile clays and loams in the lowlands, forming most of the 'permanent grassland' category of the agricultural returns at that time. It varied widely, from pastures heavily grazed throughout the year and mostly dominated by perennial rye grass to hay meadows which had a mixed regime of cutting and grazing and typically supported a wide variety of grasses and colourful herbs. Since 1940, these permanent grasslands have increasingly been subjected to agricultural improvement by ploughing and re-seeding (and often also with herbicide and fertiliser addition) with commercial strains of perennial rye-grass. Such improvement gives dominance of high production grass and virtually eliminates herbaceous weeds. The hay meadows, many of which once had high nature conservation value in their floral variety, have been particularly affected. Most of the other permanent grassland types have shown substantial, though often less abrupt, reduction in floral interest through improvement in some degree.

The process is an obvious and dramatic one to any botanist old enough to have known the countryside before 1950. It actually represents the biggest of all habitat losses which have occurred over the period of the last 45 years or so. Yet, because of the lack of earlier base-line surveys, very little information on the quantitative nature of the change is available. Only a few sample surveys have been made and all of these are quite recent, so that the scale of loss can only be inferred from the earlier observations that in many parts of the country, the majority of hay meadows up to at least 1940 had an abundance of colourful flowers.

A. Unimproved grassland
Yorkshire Dales National Park

A survey in 1981 showed that of 12,661 enclosed fields, 3,746 were hay meadows, most of the remainder being grazed permanent pastures with very little arable. Of the 3,746 hay meadows, only 185 (4·9%) could be regarded as herb-rich and only 60 had a score of indicator plant species above the level qualifying for protected area status. Of these 60 meadows, 38 are at present being considered for scheduling as SSSIs but first require re-survey to confirm that their interest has been maintained.

M. Alcock, NCC, unpublished.

Cumbria

Within a sample 10% survey of Cumbria, the proportion of grassland within enclosed farmland was 82%, the remainder being arable. Of the grassland area, 89% was classified as improved, another 8% as semi-improved and only 3% as unimproved. Within the 3% unimproved grassland (the class with significant nature conservation value), 1·5% was marshy grassland, 0·7% was neutral grassland and 0·4% was calcareous grassland. The total area of unimproved grassland within the sample was 9 sq km, of which neutral grassland covered 2 sq km.

P. Kelly, NCC, unpublished.

Old counties of Huntingdon and Peterborough (now Cambridgeshire)
A survey in 1971 showed that, of 13,544 ha of permanent grassland and rough grazings, only 356 ha (3-4%) were found to be botanically rich.

D. A. Wells, NCC, unpublished.

Worcestershire and Herefordshire
Surveys in 1982 by the two county Nature Trusts showed that, within a total of 176,191 ha of permanent enclosed grassland, 10,003 ha (5·7%) was unimproved. Figures for area of botanically interesting grassland are not available, but are certainly less than 10,000 ha.

B. Grazing marsh
This is a type of neutral grassland formed by reclamation of fen and estuarine saltings. It varies in botanical interest, but some grazing marshes are rich, and many have high interest for their birds (even when converted to arable). and for the associated drainage ditch system.

North Kent marshes
The reclaimed permanent pastures bordering the south side of the Thames estuary covered 14,750 ha in 1935. By 1982 the total area was reduced to 7,675 ha. Of this 48% loss, 13% represented urban development and mineral workings, and 35% resulted from conversion to arable.
Williams, G., Henderson. A., Goldsmith, L. and Spreadborough, A., 1983. **Wildfowl** 34, 33-47.

Fenland basin washes
During draining of the Fenland and its conversion to arable, certain riverside areas, mainly along the Rivers Ouse, Nene and Welland, were kept for flood water storage and maintained under permanent grassland. In the early 19th Century there were 6,094 ha of washlands, and much of this was still so used in 1934. With further drainage improvements they have become less needed, and conversion to arable has now reached 49%, most of which is no longer flooded in winter. The largest remaining site and the most regularly flooded is the Ouse washes (1,860 ha).
Thomas, G. J., Allen, D. A. and Grose, M. P. B., 1983. Biological Conservation (in press).

Yare basin marshes
Over an area of 20,000 ha of former grazing marsh is this outer segment of Broadland (including Halvergate Marshes) grassland covered 19,000 ha and arable < 1,000 in 1967. By 1982, 6,940 ha of the area (35%) was arable and grassland was reduced to 13,060 ha. Data on the proportion of unimproved grazing marsh in the remaining grassland is not available.
Broads Authority, evidence to House of Lords Sub-committee on Agriculture and the Environment, January 1984.

1:5 Loss of calcareous grasslands
Calcareous grassland is the semi-natural sward formed over centuries of grazing, mainly by sheep (but also rabbits) on areas of lime-rich rock. It refers especially to the open downlands of the Cretaceous chalk and Jurassic limestone stretching in broad bands across the lowlands of England. These sheep downs covered very large areas on these rock formations up to about 1800, but they were extensively ploughed to grow corn during the Napoleonic Wars (c.1815) and have been increasingly reclaimed to arable or improved grassland ever since. Quite large areas still existed in 1939, but the outbreak of World War II brought compulsory 'Cultivation Orders' which resulted in further extensive ploughing of chalk and limestone downs. After 1945, most of the remaining downlands were on scarp slopes too steep to plough, and the only large surviving areas of continuous calcareous grassland were the Ministry of Defence ranges on Salisbury Plain and Porton Down in Wiltshire.

Since 1945 reclamation of downland has continued, and the scarp remnants are no longer safe. Crawler tractors can plough steep slopes and both fertilisers and herbicides can be spread from the air. Even where grassland remains it has often been improved by enhancing nutrient levels, with the consequent loss of botanical variety and interest as grasses dominate the smaller herbs. Many downland remnants have passed out of farmed use altogether and in the present frequent absence of rabbits (post-myxomatosis, 1954-1955), coarse invasive grasses and then naturally regenerating scrub have increasingly taken over and suppressed the herbs and dwarf shrubs.

The general post-war picture has thus been of a continuing loss of open calcareous grassland and the deterioration of many remaining areas not actually ploughed. At present, quantification of these changes is limited to a few sample study areas, since background statistics on calcareous grassland are not readily available.

Dorset: chalk grassland
In 1811 there were 27,694 ha of chalk grassland. A survey in 1934 showed a minimum of 7,714 ha and possibly up to 10,000 ha remaining ('chalk grassland' is not a precise term and there are problems of definition, and thus of measurement). An accurate survey in 1967 showed that only 3,285 ha were left and a repeat in 1972 gave 2,268 ha. The loss between 1934-1972 was thus 71-77%.

C. Jones, 1973. **The conservation of chalk downland in Dorset.** Dorset County Council.

Chalk grassland in other districts
A full survey of all remaining chalk grassland, covering 16 English counties was conducted in 1966, and showed that 44,850 ha of unimproved types still remained. In 1980, samples covering 51% of this total were re-examined and showed that 21% had been lost to ploughing (61%), scrubbing over, and other changes since 1966.

J. Blackwood and C. Tubbs, NCC, unpublished.
If the 21% loss 1966-1980 is projected as a constant rate, the loss for the whole period 1940-1984 is 48%. It is, however, known from eye witness accounts (N. W. Moore, C. D. Pigott, pers. comm.) that the greatest rate of loss was from ploughing during 1940-1945. Overall losses

1940-1984 are thus likely to be closer to the 70 + % measured for Dorset. Allowing also for deterioration of a further fraction of the remaining chalk grassland either through nutrient enrichment or excessive military disturbance, it is estimated that only 20% of the area of chalk grassland present in 1940 is still of significant nature conservation interest.

1:6 Loss and damage to limestone pavements

Ward and Evans (1976) surveyed all the 537 major occurrences of limestone pavement in Britain, (mostly located in Cumbria and Yorkshire), and found that 39% of their total extent had been damaged or destroyed mainly by recent removal of stone for decorative purposes, especially rockery construction. This figure conceals the distribution of damage, for only 3% of the 537 pavements showed no detectable damage, and only 13% were considered to be 95% intact. These are minimum figures for they were collected nearly ten years ago, and stone removal from some pavements has continued, thereby increasing the extent of damage to an estimated 45%. Section 34 of the Wildlife and Countryside Act 1981 now makes specific provision for the Nature Conservancy Council and Countryside Commission to notify pavements of special interest to the local planning authority, and for the Secretary of State or relevant authority to make Limestone Pavement Orders designating such areas and prohibiting the removal of stone.

Ward, S. D. and Evans, D. F. 1976 **Conservation Assessment of British Limestone Pavements based on floristic criteria.** Biol. Conserv. 9, 217-233.

Other lowland types of peatland

Survey of lowland fens and valley mires is still in progress and figures on post-1950 losses are not yet available. The past scale of losses may be judged from the history of the draining of the East Anglian Fenland, the largest expanse of the fens which were once widespread in the lowlands.

In 1637, when major draining operations began, there were 3,380 sq. km. of swamp in the Fenland. By 1825, 2,400 sq. km. (71%) had been drained for agricultural use, and by 1934 only 100 sq. km. of fen and wet grazing marsh remained. Today, no more than 10 sq. km. of the area could be regarded as fen, and the remaining 99·7% is largely agricultural land, most of it arable.

Thomas, G. J., Allen, D. A. and Grose, M. P. B., 1983. Biological Conservation, in press.

A survey of lowland peatlands in Wales (fens, valley, basin and raised mires) showed that of 711 recorded as mire habitat in 1910, only 289 still supported significant areas of mire vegetation in 1978. This represents a 60% loss of sites during the 68-year period, without taking account of damage which has certainly occurred to some of the remaining sites.

Ratcliffe, J. B. and Hattey, R. P. (1982). Welsh Lowland Peatland Survey, Nature Conservancy Council, Research Report 431.

1:7 Loss of upland grasslands, heaths and blanket bog

The total area of uncultivated, unenclosed hill land in Britain in 1950 is estimated at 7·0-7·5 million hectares, depending on how much marginal land is included.

Since 1950, the grasslands, heaths and blanket bogs of the sub-montane zone (below the climatic upper tree limit and covering the bulk of the total area) have been replaced or modified by the following land use developments:

Afforestation

Britain had 1·312 million ha of conifer plantations in 1980, 70% established since 1950 (Centre for Agricultural Strategy Report on Forestry 1980). Most of these new plantations have been established in sub-montane upland areas, and the bulk of further new planting (continuing at c.20,000 + ha/year) will be on such ground.

Reclamation of moorland

The pushing back of the moorland edge to create more farmland has continued in most districts by enclosure, fertilising and, sometimes, ploughing and re-seeding with commercial grasses, or even conversion to arable. It is a piecemeal process and statistics are patchy. Between 1950 and 1980, the following areas of moorland were reclaimed in four National Parks: Dartmoor 4614 ha, Brecon Beacons 3822 ha, Northern Snowdonia 1143 ha, North York Moors 5480 ha, giving a total of 15,060 ha, which it is believed can be reliably extrapolated to other upland regions of England and Wales to give a total of 150,000 ha reclaimed in the last 30 years. With an approximate total area of 2 million ha of hill ground in England and Wales, this represents nearly 8% of the total. On Exmoor, MAFF data showed 23,600 ha of moorland and heath in 1947, and 18,800 ha in 1976, a 20% loss during the 31 year period. The rate of moorland reclamation over the whole of Scotland has probably averaged less than in England and Wales, but is considerable in total.

Intensified use of hill grazings

This consists of the increase of sheep stocking rates which, combined with indiscriminate moor burning, has caused the regression of dwarf shrub (mainly heather) moorland to acidic grassland, and abandonment of many grouse moors in western Britain during the last 35 years. Many areas of blanket bog have been dried out and degraded by repeated fire, and those of the southern Pennines have suffered loss of *Sphagnum* cover through industrial pollution over a longer period.

Parry, M., Bruce, A. and Harkness, C. 1981. The plight of British moorlands. New Scientist. 550-551

Deterioration of open water key sites

Lakes and rivers are seldom completely lost, but they suffer varying degrees of deterioration and reduction in nature conservation interest, and those in col. 3 above have since shown significant reduction in fauna and flora, as indicated:

In the case of most of the damaged lakes, expensive re-habilitation programmes could restore most of the interest. Many once heavily polluted rivers (e.g. Thames, Tyne, Trent) have

been very substantially 'cleaned up' since 1950
with consequent improvement in wildlife interest,
especially fish.
Data from C. Newbold, NCC (unpublished).

Annex 2

Bodies consulted

We are grateful to the following organisations and individuals who commented on the discussion paper issued in November 1983.

Anglian Water Authority
Association of County Councils
Association of Directors & River Inspectors
    of Scotland
Association of District Councils
Association of Metropolitan Authorities
Association of Welsh County Councils
C. Baines
R. E. Boote
Botanical Society of the British Isles
British Association for Shooting and Conservation
British Ecological Society
British Field Sports Society
British Trust for Conservation Volunteers
British Trust for Conservation Volunteers Scotland
British Trust for Ornithology
R. W. Cleal, Sand and Gravel Association
S. Clifford, Common Ground
Cobham Resource Consultants
Conservation Committee, Geological Society
    of London
Council for Environmental Education
Council for the Protection of Rural England
Council for the Protection of Rural Wales
Country Landowners Association
Countryside Commission
Countryside Commission for Scotland
E. B. Cowell, BP International
Lord Cranbrook
Crofters Commission
Department of Agriculture and Fisheries
    for Scotland
Department of the Environment
Eastern Council for Sport and Recreation
East of Scotland College of Agriculture
East Midlands Council for Sport and Recreation
English Tourist Board
Exmoor National Park
Farmers Union of Wales
Farming and Wildlife Advisory Group
Fauna and Flora Preservation Society
Forestry Commission
Game Conservancy
Greater London Council
Greater London and South East Council
    for Sport & Recreation
S. H. Greenan, Isle of Wight County Council
P. V. Hazel, County Planning Department,
    Hampshire
Highlands and Islands Development Board
Industry Department for Scotland
Institute of Biology
Institute of Terrestrial Ecology
International Waterfowl Research Bureau
H. H. Jones, County Planning Officer, Powys

A. King, Common Ground
V. Koester, Ministry of the Environment, Denmark
Lake District National Park
Land Authority for Wales
Landscape Institute
R. G. A. Lofthouse, Standing Committee on
    Countryside Sports
London Wildlife Trust
Marine Conservation Society
Prof. K. Mellanby
Mid Wales Development Corporation
Ministry of Agriculture, Fisheries and Food
Ministry of Defence
National Farmers Union
National Farmers Union of Scotland
National Museum of Wales
National Trust
National Trust for Scotland
Natural Environment Research Council
E. M. Nicholson
North of Scotland College of Agriculture
Northumbria Water Authority
North West Water Authority
North Yorks Moors National Park
Peak District National Park
Pembrokeshire Coast National Park
Red Deer Commission
J-P. Ribaut, Council of Europe
Royal Forestry Society of England, Wales
    and Northern Ireland
Royal Geographical Society
Royal Geological Society
Royal Institute of British Architects
Royal Institution of Chartered Surveyors
Royal Society
Royal Society for Nature Conservation
    — on behalf of County Trusts and Watch Trust
Royal Society for the Protection of Birds
Royal Town Planning Institute
Royal Zoological Society of Scotland
K. Runcie, East of Scotland College of Agriculture
Scottish Branch, Royal Institution
    of Chartered Surveyors
Scottish Civic Trust
Scottish Development Department
Scottish Environmental Education Committee
Scottish Landowners Federation
Scottish Tourist Board
Scottish Wildlife Trust
Soil Association
South West Council for Sport and Recreation
Southern Water Authority
South West Water Authority
Sports Council
Sports Council for Wales
Staffordshire County Council Countryside
    Sub-committee
A. T. Swindall on behalf of the
    County Planning Officers' Society

W. J. Syratt, BP International
Timber Growers Scotland
Timber Growers UK
Thames Water Authority
University College London, Staff and Students of
    MSc Course in Conservation
Urban Wildlife Group
Wales Tourist Board
Welsh Development Agency
Welsh Office
Welsh Water Authority
Wessex Water Authority
West Glamorgan County Planning Committee
Wildfowl Trust
Wildlife Link — on behalf of members
J. Workman, consultant on conservation and
    forestry to the National Trust
World Wildlife Fund
Yorkshire and Humberside Council for Sport
    and Recreation
Yorkshire Dales National Park
Yorkshire Water Authority

Annex 3

Holyhead coast (page 46).
The Holyhead coast shows an important range of features of considerable value to structural geology.

Vallis Vale (page 46).
An important geological site of historic interest and one which has been recently restored by the NCC.

Herb rich hay meadow (page 50), **Chalk grassland at Porton Down** (page 51) and **Acidic lowland heath, Dorset** (page 52). These are types of habitats referred to in 12.2.1.

Sand lizard (page 53).
An endangered species of acidic lowland heaths and sand dunes.

Hart's-tongue fern (page 54).
A characteristic plant of vertical crevices (grikes) in limestone pavement.

Limestone pavement, Gait Barrows NNR (page 54).
Another of the habitats referred to in 12.2.1 that have declined rapidly since 1940.

White admiral (page 55).
A characteristic butterfly of southern woodlands with honeysuckle on which the eggs are laid.

Lady Park Wood, Wye valley (page 55).
High forest of mixed broad-leaf trees with well developed field layer.

Wood anemones and celandines (page 55).
Two woodland plants which flourish under condition of good light penetration through the canopy.

Calthorpe Broad, Norfolk (page 57).
Gradation from aquatic vegetation through swamp to carr woodland. Aquatic communities of this kind in Broadland have largely disappeared through water pollution.

Bogbean (page 57).
A typical plant of both lowland and moorland bogs and swamps which has become rarer in some areas through wetland draining.

Heather moorland in north-east Scotland (page 59).
An example of the grouse moors which form an important upland wildlife habitat. They are subject to afforestation, agricultural reclamation and reduction in heather through intensive sheep grazing.

Salt-marsh and sand dunes on the north Norfolk coast (page 60).
Coastal habitats subject to drainage and loss through reclamation, recreation and afforestation.

Sea-aster (page 60).
A typical plant of estuarine saltmarshes.

Estuarine reclamation in the Wash (page 60).
Construction of sea walls allows conversion of saltmarsh and mudflat to farmland, first as grazing marsh grassland, but, increasingly nowadays, to arable.

Swallowtail butterfly (page 61).
The largest British butterfly, which has evolved into a different race from that on the continent of Europe. Formerly more widespread in lowland England fens, but is now restricted to the Norfolk Broads.

Four-spotted libellula (page 62).
One of the most widespread and least threatened of British dragonflies.

Tree lungwort (page 62).
One of the largest and most conspicuous British lichens, and one which is particularly sensitive to acidification through atmospheric pollution. It has disappeared from a wide radius round the major industrial areas and is still declining in parts of western Britain.

Common snipe (page 63).
A once common breeding bird of wet lowland meadow which has declined dramatically through draininig, although it is still widespread in the uplands.

Stone-curlew (page 63).
A bird of open-steppe country which once nested as far north as the Yorkshire wolds, but has retreated and declined as chalk downlands have been ploughed and enclosed and the East Anglian brecks have been afforested.

Pine marten (page 63).
A very local mammal of the northern mountains and woodlands which has expanded its range in recent years, although it has become rarer in the Lake District and Snowdonia.

Early spider-orchid (page 64).
A rare orchid of southern chalk downs which has declined markedly through reclamation and scrubbing-over of the habitat and through collecting. It is specially protected by law as an endangered species.

Snake's-head fritillary (page 64).
One of the most characteristic plants of southern, lowland meadows, once widespread and abundant, but now reduced to scattered and isolated colonies in much need of protection. Its decline has resulted from the extensive improvement in lowland meadows as described in 12.2.1.1.

Woodland on Taynish NNR (page 65).
An example of original native oak woodland which has persisted in more or less its present form for thousands of years and has developed a varied flora and fauna that is immediately modified by clear felling; further loss occurs if the woodland cover is not restored or is replaced by conifers.

Lichens on tree-trunk, Taynish NNR (page 65).
An example of the varied communities of large lichens which grow on the trunks of trees in western native woodland and which are of great international interest. They are an important element in the associated flora which is reduced if the original woodland cover is lost.

Bure Marshes NNR (page 66).
An example of remaining fen and carr woodland in the Norfolk Broads; the habitat of the swallowtail butterfly.

Tuddenham Heath (page 66).
A lowland acidic heathland with heather, extensively colonised by birch to form woodland: the characteristic habitat of the nightjar.

Wye NNR (page 66).
A surviving area of chalk grassland in Kent, the habitat of numerous rare and declining plants and animals, notably orchids and butterflies such as the early spider-orchid and Adonis blue butterfly.

Coed Ganllwyd (page 67).
Sessile oakwood in the valleys of the north Wales mountains. The humid climate, proximity of waterfalls and woodland shade give a profusion of mosses, liverworts, lichens and ferns on the blocks and rock outcrops and on the trees themselves.

Rannoch Moor, NNR (page 67).
Blanket bog with bogbean pools and sphagnum 'lawns': the habitat of the Rannoch rush and the greenshank. Mountain habitats in the high mountain ranges behind.

Experimental Plots, Monks Wood (page 68).
Wild flowers are grown for seed at Monks Wood Experimental Station as part of the NCC's contract with Institute of Terrestrial Ecology to develop means of establishing herb-rich swards similar to those in the herb-rich hay meadows which are now so uncommon.

Blanket afforestation in Galloway (page 77).
The extensive planting of large continuous blocks of conifers transforms open moorland with its associated plants and animals to closed forest with a contrasting flora and fauna.

Agricultural landscape in the Chilterns (page 79).
A typical agricultural landscape in the centre of lowland England which superficially appears to offer considerable scope for wildlife but which, in practice, contains mainly a range of habitats impoverished through modern land-use practices.

Muir of Dinnet NNR (page 84).
A varied habitat complex of moorland, lake and forest in Aberdeenshire.

Southern marsh-orchid (page 84).
A declining orchid of lowland fens and wet meadows.

Tees Valley (page 87).
An example of an area which, without contrasting features of outstanding nature conservation importance, nevertheless contains in total a wide variety of habitats, plants and animals, representing significant interest as part of the wider countryside.

Burnt Island, St. Agnes, Scilly (page 89).
The Isles of Scilly, Britain's south-west archipelago, are a classic marine site where many south-western species are found in abundance; boulder shores and sand flats are particularly rich in marine life.

Cup-coral, *Leptopsammia pruvoti* (page 89).
This, the largest and most colourful cup-coral present in British waters, is a Mediterranean-Atlantic species found in only a few sites in south-west Britain (seen here on a sheltered rock-face in deep water off the east coast of St. Mary's, Isles of Scilly).

Research on peat bog (page 90).
Research scientist recording water levels in plastic pipes from a walk-way fixed above the mire surface.

Abernethy Forest SSSI (page 94).
Legislation under the 1981 Act refers especially to site safeguard through the provision for notifying Sites of Special Scientific Interest, and through species protection which includes special measures for endangered plant and animal species such as the spring gentian.

White-fronted geese (page 95).
There is a special international obligation for Britain to safeguard those species for which a large proportion of the total world or European population migrates to Britain for a part of the year.

Ford Hall Green nature reserve, Stoke (page 96).
Even the city may contain splendid wildlife habitats on ground which has been left unused or allowed to go to waste, provided it is managed in the interest of wild plants and animals.

Kirkby Moor nature reserve (page 98).
Grant-aid from the NCC has allowed the Lincolnshire Trust for Nature Conservation to control the water levels more effectively and

provide suitable habitats for the many species which originally occurred in the ditch system.

Dolebury Warren (page 99).
Grants by NCC towards land-purchase and fencing work have enabled the National Trust, in partnership with the Avon Wildlife Trust, to safeguard and manage this nationally important limestone grassland site in the Mendip hills.

Photographs supplied by: NCC, Ardea, E. Hosking, ITE, Frank Lane, S & O Matthews, NHPA and Nature Photographers.